THE
THREEFOLD COMMONWEALTH

THE
THREEFOLD
COMMONWEALTH

Authorized Translation by E. Bowen-Wedgwood

BY
RUDOLF STEINER
Author of "The Social Future," "World Economy"

ANTHROPOSOPHIC PRESS, Inc.   NEW YORK

A746064

Copyright, 1922,
By RUDOLF STEINER

Set up and electrotyped. Published September, 1922
Reprinted November, 1943.

FERRIS PRINTING COMPANY
NEW YORK

A FOREWORD AS TO THE PURPOSE OF THIS BOOK

The social life of the present day presents grave and far-reaching problems. We are confronted by demands for social reconstruction, which shew that the solution of these problems must be sought along paths unthought-of hitherto. Borne out by the actual events of the hour, the time has perhaps come for someone to gain a hearing, who is forced by life's experience to maintain, that the neglect to turn our thoughts into the paths that are now needed has stranded us in confusion and perplexity. It is under that conviction that this book is written. Its purpose is to discuss what needs doing, in order that those demands, which are being urged by a large part of .mankind to-day, may be turned in the direction of a determinate social will and purpose.

Personal likes and dislikes should enter but little into the formation of a social purpose. The demands, welcome or un-welcome, are there; and they must be reckoned with as facts of social life. This should be borne in mind by those who, from their personal situation in life, may be inclined to be annoyed at the author's way of discussing the demands of the working-class, because in their opinion he lays too one-sided a stress on these de-mands, as on something that must be reck-oned with when determining on a social purpose. But what the author wants, is to present life as it exists to-day in all its full reality, in so far as he is able from his knowledge of it. He has ever before his eyes the fatal consequences that must ensue, if people refuse to see facts, which are actually there, which have arisen out of the life of modern mankind,—and if they accordingly persist in ignoring a social will and purpose in which these facts find their place.

Those people again will not be pleased with the author's remarks, who regard themselves as experts in practical life,—or in what, under the influence of fond habit, has come to be regarded as practical life. They will be of opinion, that whoever wrote this book was not a practical person. These are just the people, who, in the author's opinion, have everything to unlearn and re-learn. Their practice of life seems to him the very thing, which is demonstrated by the actual facts from which mankind are suffering to be an utter mistake,—that very mistake that has led to boundless and immeasurable fatalities. These people will be obliged to recognise the practicability of much that has seemed to them absurd idealism. And although they may condemn this book at the outset, because its opening pages say less about the economic than about the spiritual life of modern mankind, yet the author's

own acquaintance with life forces him to
the conviction, that, unless people can bring
themselves to pay due and accurate attention to the spiritual life of modern mankind, they will only go on adding fresh
mistakes to the old ones.

Neither will what is said in these pages
altogether please those, who are for ever
repeating with endless variations the
phrases: that man must rise above ab-
sorption in purely material interests,—
that he must turn to "ideals," to the things
of the "spirit." For the author does not
attach much importance to mere references
to the "spirit" or to talk about a vague
spiritual world. The only spirituality he
can acknowledge, is that which forms the
substance of man's own life and manifests
its power no less in mastering the practical
problems of life than in constructing a
philosophy of life and of the universe,
which can satisfy the needs of man's soul.
The important point, is not the knowledge,
—or supposed knowledge,—of a spiritual
life, but that such a spiritual life shews it-

self in a practical grip of realities, and is
not a special preserve for the inner life
of the soul, a backwater alongside the full
tide of realities.

And so, what is said in these pages will
seem to the "spiritually-minded" too un-
spiritual, to "practical persons" too remote
from practice. But the author's view is,
that he may have his own special use at
the present time, for the very reason, that
he neither tends towards that aloofness
from life, which is to be found in many a
man who thinks himself practical, nor yet
can hold in any way with the kind of talk
about the spirit, which conjures up a mir-
age out of words.

It is as a question of economics, of human rights and of the spirit, that the social
question is discussed in this book. The
author thinks that he perceives, how the
true form of the social question emerges
as an outcome of the requirements of the
economic life, the life of "rights" and the
spiritual life. Through such a perception
alone can the impulses come, which shall

make it possible to give these three
branches of social life a shape that permits
of healthy life within the social order.   In
the earlier ages of mankind's evolution, the
social   instincts   secured   these   three
branches being woven together in the
whole life of society in a manner adapted
to human nature at that period.   At the
present stage of his evolution, man is faced
with the necessity of working out this
combination of function by conscious, determinate social will and purpose.   Between those earlier ages and the present, in
the countries where the question of a social purpose is most immediate, we find the
old instincts and the new consciousness
overlapping and playing through one another in a fashion quite inadequate to the
needs of modern mankind.   In a great deal
of social thinking, which people believe to
be clear-sighted and conscious, the old instincts are still at work and enfeeble men's
thought for dealing with urgent facts.   It
requires a much more radical effort than
is usually supposed, for the man of the

present day to work his way out of the husks of what is dead and done with.

One must first be willing to recognise this fully, before, in the author's opinion, it is possible to see the forms that industrial economy, human rights, and spiritual life must take, in order to be in keeping with a healthy social life such as the new age demands. What the author feels called on to say as to the lines that these new forms must inevitably follow, is submitted to the judgment of the day in the following pages. The author's desire, is to give the first impetus along a path, that shall lead to social ends in keeping with the actual realities and exigencies of life at the present time; for he believes, that it is only through effort thus directed that our social will and purpose can get beyond mere utopianism and wordy sentiment.

And if anyone still thinks that this book has somewhat of a utopian character, the author would ask him to consider the pictures which people draw in their own

xii   FOREWORD

minds of the kind of society that they look
to see arise,—how very wide of life such
pictures are, and how apt to degenerate
into mere moonshine. That is the very
reason, why, when these people do meet
with something that is drawn from actual
reality and experience,—as attempted
here,—they regard it as a utopia. To
many persons, nothing is "concrete" outside their own customary line of thought;
and so the concrete itself is to them an ab-
straction, when they are unaccustomed to
think it.(§)—Hence they will think this
book abstract.

Beginning of April, 1919

(§) The author in the following pages has deliber-
ately avoided confining himself to the terms in common
use in standard treatises on political economy. He
knows quite well the places which a technical economist
will pick out as being amateurish. But he has selected
his mode of expression, partly because he desires to
address himself also to persons who are not familiar
with the literature of sociology and economics, but
chiefly, because it is his opinion, that most of what is
peculiarly technical in such writings will be shewn by a
new age to be partial and defective, even in the very
form of its expression.
It may also be thought, that some reference should
have been made by the author to other persons, whose
social ideas bear an incidental resemblance to his own.

With people again, whose minds are harnessed hard and fast to a party-pro-
gramme, the author's views will at first
find no favour. Of this he is well aware.
Still he believes, that it will not be long
before many party men come to the conclusion, that the actual facts of evolution
have got far beyond the programmes of
the parties, and that it is urgently necessary to free oneself from all such party-
programmes and to form an independent
opinion as to the immediate objectives of
the social will and purpose.

It must however be remembered, that in the whole conception here put forward,—a conception which the author
believes he owes to long years of practical experience,
—the essential point is not whether a particular thought
has taken this or that form, but what one takes as one's
starting-ground, and the road one pursues in giving
practical realisation to the impulses which underlie this
conception. As may be seen from Chapter IV, the
author was already doing what he could to get these
ideas practically realised, at a time when ideas that
look in some respect similar had as yet attracted no
attention

THE THREEFOLD COMMON-WEALTH

Introductory Preface to the New Edition of 1920

The problems presented by social life for solution in our times can be understood by nobody who approaches them with the thought of any kind of utopia in his mind. One's views and sentiments may lead one to the belief, that certain institutions, which one has mapped out according to one's own ideas, must be for the happiness of mankind. This belief may carry all the force of passionate conviction; and yet one may be talking quite wide of the actual social question, when one tries to obtain practical recognition for what one believes.

One will find this assertion hold true at
the present day, even when pushed to what
may appear an absurd extreme. Suppose,
for instance, somebody possessed a perfect theoretical solution of the social question, he might nevertheless be acting on
an utterly unpractical conviction, if he
tried to press this carefully thought-out
solution upon mankind. For we are no
longer living in an age, when one is justified in believing that public life can be affected in such a way. Men's souls are differently constituted; and they could never
say about public affairs: Here is somebody who understands the social institutions that are needed; we will take his
opinion and act on it. Ideas concerning
social life simply cannot be brought home
to people after this fashion; and it is a
fact that is fully recognised in this book,
which is already known to a fairly large
public. Those who have set it down as
utopian, have totally missed its whole aim
and intention. Especially has this been
the case with those, who themselves cling

to a utopian form of thought:—they attribute to the other person what is essentially their own mental characteristic. A practical thinker to-day recognises as one of the experiences of public life, that nothing can be done with an utopian idea, however convincing it may be in appearance. Nevertheless, many people have some idea of this type, which they feel impelled to bring before their fellow-men, especially in the field of economics. They will be forced to recognise that their words are wasted. Their fellow-men can find no use for what they have to offer.

This should be treated as a piece of practical experience; for it points to a fact of importance in public life: namely, the remoteness of people's thoughts from real life:—how wide their thoughts are from what reality,—economic reality for instance,—demands.

Can one hope to master the tangled intricacies of public affairs, if one brings to them a mode of thought alto-

gether remote from life? This
question is not one likely to find general
favour; for it involves the admission that
one's way of thought *is* remote from life.
Yet, until this admission is made, it is not
possible to approach the other question—
the *social one*. For the remoteness of
thought from life is a question of grave
concern for the whole modern civilised
world; and only when people treat it as
such will they see light as to what is needed
for social life.

This question brings us to the consideration of the form taken by modern spiritual
life. Modern man has evolved a spiritual
life, which is to a very great degree dependent on state institutions and on economic forces. The human being is brought
whilst still a child under the education and
instruction of the state; and he can be educated only in the way permitted by the industrial and economic conditions of the environment from which he springs.

It might easily be supposed, that this
would ensure a person's being well quali-

fied for the conditions of life at the present day, for that the state must possess every opportunity of arranging the whole system of education and instruction (which constitutes the essential part of public spiritual life) in the best interests of the human community. It might well be supposed too, that the way to make a person the best possible member of the human community is to educate him in accordance with the economic opportunities of the environment from which he comes, and then pass him on, thus educated, to fill one of the openings that these opportunities afford him. —It devolves upon this book,—an unpopular task to-day,—to shew, that the chaotic condition of our public life, comes from the spiritual life's dependence on the State and on industrial economy—and to shew further, that one part of the burning social question is the emancipation of spiritual life from this dependence.

This involves attacking very widespread errors. That the State should take over the whole system of education, has long been regarded as a beneficial step in human progress; and persons of a socialistic turn of mind find it difficult to conceive of anything else, than that society should educate the individual to its service according to its own standards.

People are loathe to recognise, what nevertheless, in this field, it is absolutely necessary should be recognised; namely, that in the process of man's historic evolution a thing, that at an earlier period was all right, may at a later period become all wrong.   In order that a new age might come about in human affairs, it was necessary that the whole system of education, and with it public spiritual life, should be removed from those circles that had exclusive possession of it all through the middle ages, and entrusted to the State.   But to continue to maintain this state of things, is a grave social mistake.

This is what the first part of the book is intended to shew.   The spiritual life has matured to freedom within the framework of the state; but it cannot rightly

enjoy and exercise this freedom unless it
is granted complete self-government. The
whole character assumed by the spiritual
life requires that it should form a completely independent branch of the body social. The educational and teaching system,
lying as it does at the root of all spiritual
life, must be put under the management
of those people who are educating and
teaching; and none of the influences at
work in state or industry should have any
say or interference in this management.
No teacher should spend more time on
teaching than will allow of his also being
a manager in his own sphere of activity.
And in the way that he himself conducts
the teaching and education, so too he will
conduct the management. Nobody will issue
instructions, who is not at the same time
actively engaged in teaching and educating. No parliament has any voice in it,—
nor any individual, who once on a time
may have taught, but is no longer personally teaching. The experience learnt at
first hand in actual teaching passes direct

into the management.—In such a system, practical knowledge and efficiency must, of course, tell in the very highest possible degree.

It may no doubt be objected, that even under such a selfgoverning spiritual life things will not be quite perfect. But then, in real life, that is not to be looked for. All one can aim at, is the best that is possible. With each child of man there are new abilities growing up, and these will really be passed on into the life of the community, when the care of developing them rests entirely with people who can judge and decide on spiritual grounds alone. How far a particular child should be brought on in one direction or another, can only be judged in a spiritual community that is quite free and detached. What steps should be taken to ensure their decision having its "rights," this too is a matter only to be determined by a free spiritual community. From such a community the State and the economic life can receive the forces they need, and which they cannot

get of themselves when they fashion spiritual life from their own points of view.

It follows from the whole tenor of the
following pages, that the directors of the
free spiritual life will have charge also of
the arrangements and course of teaching in
those institutes also, which are specially
directed to the service of the State or of
the economic world.—Law-schools, Trades-
schools, Agricultural and Industrial Colleges, would all take their form from the
free spiritual life. Many prejudices are
bound to be aroused, when the principles
stated in this book are pursued to these,
their right consequences. But from what
do such prejudices proceed? The anti-
social spirit in them becomes evident, when
one recognises, that at bottom they proceed from an unconscious persuasion, that
people connected with education must necessarily be unpractical persons, remote
from life,—not the sort of people whom
one could for a moment expect to institute
arrangements that would be of any real
use for the practical departments of life,

and that all such arrangements must be instituted by the people actively engaged in practical life, whilst the educators must work on the lines laid down for them.

In thinking like this, people do not see, that the educators need to fix their lines of work themselves, from the smallest things up to the biggest, that it is when they cannot do so that they grow unpractical and remote from life. And then you may give them any principle to work on, laid down by apparently the most practical persons, and yet their education will not turn out people really practically equipped for life. Our anti-social conditions are brought about, because people are turned out into social life not educated to feel socially. People with social feelings can only come from a mode of education that is directed and carried on by persons who themselves feel socially. The *social* question will never be touched, until the education question and the question of the spiritual life are treated as a vital part of it. An anti-social spirit is created not merely by economic institutions, but through the attitude of the human beings within these institutions being an anti-social one. And it is anti-social, to have the young brought up and taught by persons, who themselves are made strangers to real life by having their lines of work and the substance of their work laid down for them from outside.

The State establishes law-schools. And it requires, that the substance of the jurisprudence taught in these law-schools should be the same as the State has fixed for its own constitution and administration, from its own points of view. When the law-schools proceed wholly from a free spiritual life, this free spiritual life itself will supply the substance of the jurisprudence taught in them. The State will wait to take its mandate from the spiritual life. It will be fertilised by the reception of living ideas, such as can issue only from a spiritual life that is free.

But the human-beings, growing up to life, are within the spiritual domain, and will go forth with views of their own to put into practice. The education given by people who are strangers to life, inside educational institutes planned by mere practicians,—this is not an education that can be realised in practice. The only teaching that can find practical realisation comes from teachers who understand life and its practice from a point of view of their own. In this book an attempt is made to give at least a sketch of the way in which a free spiritual organisation will shape its details of working.

In Utopian minds, the book will rouse all manner of questions. Artists and other spiritual workers will anxiously ask whether genius will find itself better off in the free spiritual life than in the one at present provided by the State and the economic powers? In putting such questions, however, they must please to remember, that the book is in no respect intended to be Utopian. Hence it never lays down a hard and fast theory. This must be so and so, or so and so.

Its aim is to promote the formation of such forms of human social life, as, from their joint working shall lead to desirable conditions. And anyone, who judges life from experience, and not from theoretic prejudice, will say to himself "When there is a free spiritual community, whose dealings with life are guided by its own lights, then anyone who is creating out of his own free genius will have a prospect of his creations being duly appreciated."

The "social question" is not a thing that has cropped up at this particular point in the life of man, which can be solved straight away by a handful of people, or by parliaments, and, once solved, will remain solved. It is an integral part of our new civilised life; and it has come to stay. It will have to be solved afresh for each moment of the world's historic evolution. For man's life has entered with this new age upon a phase, when what starts by being a social institution turns ever and again into something *anti*-social, which has each time continually to be overcome

afresh. Just as an organic body, when it
has once been fed and satisfied, passes after
a while into a state of hunger again, so
the body social passes from one state of
order again into disorder. There is no
more a panacea for keeping social conditions in good order, than there is a food
that will satisfy the body for ever and always. Men can however enter into forms
of community, which, through their joint
action in actual life, will bring man's existence constantly back into the social path.
And one of these forms of community is
the self-governing spiritual branch of the
body social.

All the experiences of the present time
make it plain, that what is socially needed
is, for the spiritual life *free self-administration,* and for the economic life *associative labour.* Industrial economy in modern
human life is made up of the production
of commodities, circulation of commodities and consumption of commodities.
These are the processes for satisfying human wants; and human beings and their

activities are involved in these processes. Each has his own part-interest in them; each must take such a share in them as he is able. What any individual actually needs, only he himself alone can know and feel. As to what he himself should perform, this will be judged by him according to his measure of insight into the mutual life of the whole. It was not always so; nor is it so to-day all the world over; but in the main it is so amongst the at present civilised portion of the Earth's inhabitants. Economic evolution has kept widening its circles in the course of mankind's evolution. Household economy, once self-contained, has developed into town economy, and this again into State economy. To-day we stand before world economy. No doubt, in the New much still lingers on of the Old; and much that existed in the Old was already a forecast of the New but the above evolutionary order is the one that has become paramount in certain relations of life, and the destinies of mankind are conditioned by it.

It is altogether a wrong-headed notion to aim at organising the economic forces into an abstract world-community. Private economic organisations have, in the course of evolution, become to a very great extent merged in State economic organisations. But the State communities were created by other forces than the purely economic ones; and the endeavour to transform the State communities into economic communities is just what has brought about the social chaos of these latter times. Economic life is struggling to take the form its own peculiar forces give it, independent of State institutions, and independent also of State lines of thought. It is only possible through the growth of Associations, having their rise in purely economic considerations, and drawn jointly from circles of consumers, traders and producers. The actual conditions of life will of themselves regulate the size and scope of these Associations. Over-small Associations would prove too expensive in the working; over-large ones would get be-

yond economic grasp. The needs of life
as they arise will shew each Association the
best way of establishing interconnections
with the others. There need be no fear,
that anyone, who has to spend his life mov-
ing about from place to place, will be in
any way hampered by Associations of this
kind. He will find removing from one
group to another quite easy, when it is not
managed by the State-organisations, but
by the economic interests. One can conceive
possible arrangements within such an associative system, that would work with the
facility of a money-currency.

Within any single Association, where
there is practical sense and technical
knowledge, a very general harmony of interests can prevail. The production, circulation and consumption of goods will
not be regulated by laws, but by the persons themselves, from their own direct insight and interests. People's own active
share in the life of the Associations will
enable them to acquire the necessary insight; and the fact, that the various inter-

ests are obliged to contract a mutual balance, will ensure the goods circulating at their proper relative values. This sort of agreed combination, determined by economic considerations, is not the same as the form of combination that exists in the modern trades-unions. The activities of the modern trades-unions are expended in the economic field; but the unions are not framed primarily according to economic considerations. They are modelled on the principles taken from practical familiarity in modern times with political considerations, considerations of state. They are parliamentary bodies, where people debate, not where they come together to consider economic aspects and agree on the services to be reciprocally rendered. In these Associations, it will not be "wage-workers" sitting, using their power to get the highest possible wages out of the work-employer; it will be hand-workers, co-operating with the spiritual workers, who direct production, and with those interested in consuming the product, to effect a balance between one form of service and another, through an adjustment of prices. This is not a thing that can be done by general debate in parliamentary assemblies. One must beware of these. For who would ever be at work, if an endless number of people had to spend their time negotiating about the work! Everything will take place by agreement between man and man, between one Association and another, whilst the work goes on alongside. For this, all that is necessary is, that the joint agreement should be in accordance with the inside knowledge of the workers and with the interests of the consumers.

In saying this, one depicts no Utopia. No particular way is laid down in which this or that matter must be settled. All that is done, is to point out how people will settle matters for themselves, when once they set about working in forms of community which are in accordance with their special insight and interests.

There are two things that operate to bring men together into communities of this kind: The one, is human nature,—for it is nature that gives men wants. Or, again, a free spiritual life, for this engenders the insight that finds scope in communal life. Anyone, who bases his thoughts on reality, will admit, that Associative communities of this kind can spring up at any time, that there is nothing utopian about them. There is nothing to hinder their springing up, except that the thought of "organisation" has been so suggested into the man of the present day, that he is obsessed with the notion of organising industrial and economic life from outside. In direct contrast to such organising of men for the combined work of production, is this other kind of economic organisation, that rests on voluntary, free Association. Through this mutual Association, one man establishes ties with another; and the orderly scheme of the whole is the resultant of what each individual finds reasonable for himself.

It may of course be said: What is the use of a man, who has no property, Asso-

ciating himself with a man, who has? It
might seem better for all production and
consumption to be regulated "fairly" from
outside. But such organising kind of regulation checks the flow of free individual
creative power, through which economic
life is fed, and cuts the economic life off
from what this source alone can give it.
Putting aside any pre-conclusions, just
make the experiment of an Association between those, who to-day have no property,
and those who have; and, if no forces other
than economic ones intervene, it will be
found that the "Haves" are obliged to render the "Have-nots" service for service.
The common talk about such things to-
day does not proceed from those instincts
of life, that experience teaches, but from
certain attitudes of mind, that have arisen
out of class or other interests, not out of
economic ones. Such attitudes of mind
had a chance to grow up, because, in these
latter times, just when economic life especially was becoming more and more com-
plicated, the purely economic ideas were

unable to keep pace with it. The cramped and fettered spiritual life has acted as a drag. The people, who are carrying on economic life, are fast caught in life's routine; they are unable to see the forces that are at work shaping the world's industrial economy. They work on, without any insight into the totality of human life. But, in the Associations, one person will learn from another what it is necessary that he should know. A collective experience of economic possibilities will arise from the combined judgment of individuals, who each have insight and experience in their own particular departments.

Whilst, then, in the free spiritual life the only forces at work are those inherent to the spiritual life itself, so in an economic system modelled on associative lines, the only values that count will be those economic values that grow up under the Associations. The particular part that any individual has to play in economic life will become clear to him from actual life and work along with his economic associates.

And the weight that he carries in the general economic system will be exactly proportionate to the service he renders within it. There will be those who are unfitted to render service; and how these find their place in the general economy of the body social is discussed in the course of the book. In an economic system, that is shaped by economic forces alone, it is possible for the weak to find shelter against the strong.

Thus the body social falls apart into two independent branches, which are able to afford each other mutual support owing to the very fact, that each has its own special method of working, shaped by the forces inherent to itself. But between these two must come a third, whose life lies betwixt both. This is the true "state" branch of the body social. Here all those things find a place that must depend upon the judgment and sentiments of every person who is of age to have a voice. Within the free spiritual life, everyone busies himself according to his special abilities. Within the economic life, each fills the place that falls to him through his connection with the rest of the associative network. Within the political state-life of "rights," each comes into his own as a human being, and stands on his simple human value, in so far as this is apart from the abilities which he exercises within the free spiritual life, and independent too of whatever value that the associative economic system may set upon the goods he produces.

Hours of labour and modes of labour are shewn in this book to be matters for the political "Rights-life," for the state. Here, every man meets his fellow on an equal footing, because, here, all transactions and all control are confined to those fields of life in which all men alike are competent to form an opinion. It is the branch of the body social where men's rights and duties are adjusted.

The unity of the whole body social will spring from the separate, free expansion of its three functions. In the course of the book it is shewn, what form the energies of capital and of the means of production, as well as the use of land, may take under the joint action of these three functions of the social organism.   To someone, who is bent on "solving" the social question by a device of economics, by some economic scheme that has come up or been thought out on paper,—to him this book will seem unpractical.   But anyone, who is trying from life's experience to promote forms of combination amongst men, in which they may be able to see. what the social problems, and duties are, and how best to fulfil them,—he may perhaps admit, that the writer of this book is endeavouring after a genuine working-practice of life.

The book was first published in April, 1919.   Since then, I have published a series of articles, explanatory and supplementary to it, which have now appeared as a separate volume. (§)

It may be thought, that in both books a

(§) *An English translation of this supplementary volume is in preparation.* (Translator's note.)

great deal is said about the paths that should be pursued in social life, and very little about the "ultimate ends" of the social movement. Anyone, who thinks along the lines of life, knows, that, as a matter of fact, particular ends may present themselves in various forms. It is only those who live in abstract thoughts, who see things in single outline, and who often find fault with the person in practical life for not putting them definitely, "clearly" enough. There are many such abstractionists to be found amongst people who pride themselves on their practicality. They do not reflect, that life can assume the most manifold forms. It is a flowing tide; and if one would travel with it, one must adapt oneself even in thought and feeling to the flux that is its constant feature. Thought of this kind alone can seize and keep its hold on social problems.

It is from the observation of life that the ideas in this book have been won; it is from the observation of life that they ask to be understood.

I.

The True Shape of the Social Question, As Shewn in the Life of Modern Man

Does not the modern social movement stand revealed by the great catastrophe of the war, demonstrating in actual *facts* how inadequate the *thoughts* were, which for years have been supposed sufficient to an understanding of the working-class movement and its purport?

It is a question forced upon us by the demands of the workers and all that these involve,—demands which formerly were kept in suppression, but which at the present time are forcing their way to the surface of life. The powers that were instrumental in suppression are partially destroyed; and the position they took up towards the forces of social growth in a large part of mankind is one that nobody can wish to maintain, who does not totally fail to recognise how indestructible such impulses of human nature are.

The greatest illusions in respect to these social forces have been harboured by persons, whose situation in life gave them the power, by word and voice, either to assist or to check those influences in European life, which, in 1914, were rushing us into the catastrophe of war. These persons actually believed, that a military victory for their country would hush the mutterings of the social storm. They have since been obliged to recognise, that it was the consequences of their own attitude that first brought these social tendencies fully to light. Indeed, the present catastrophe,—which is the catastrophe of mankind,—has shewn itself to be the very event, through which, historically, these tendencies gained the opportunity to make themselves felt in their full force. During these last fateful years, both the leading persons and the

leading classes have been constantly
obliged to tune their own behaviour to the
note sounded in socialist circles. Could
they have disregarded the tone of these
circles, they would often gladly have acted
differently. And the effects of this live on
in the form which events are taking to-
day.

And now the thing, which for years past
has been drawing on in mankind's life-
evolution, preparing its way before it, has
arrived at a decisive stage,—and now
comes the tragedy: The facts are with
us in all their ripeness, but the thoughts
that came up with the growth of the facts
are no match for them. There are many
persons who trained their thoughts on the
lines of the growing process, hoping thereby to serve the social ideal which they recognised in it; and these persons find themselves to-day practically powerless before
the problems which the accomplished facts
present, and on which the destinies of
mankind hang. A good many of these persons, it is true, still believe that the things

they have so long thought necessary to
the remodelling of human life will now be
realised, and will then prove powerful
enough to give these facts a possible turn
and meet their requirements. One may
dismiss the opinion of those, who, even
now, are still under the delusion, that it
must be possible to maintain the old scheme
of things against the new demands that
are being urged by a large part of mankind. We may confine ourselves to exam-
ining what is going on in the wills of those
people who are convinced that a remodelling of social life is necessary. Even so,
we shall be forced to own to ourselves,
that party shibboleths go wandering up
and down amongst us like the dessicated
corpses of once animate creeds,—everywhere flouted and set at naught by the
evolution of facts. The facts call for deci-
sions, for which the creeds of the old parties are all unprepared. These parties certainly evolved along with the facts,—but
they, and their habits of thought, have not
kept pace with the facts. One may per-

haps venture without presumption to hold,
—in the face of still common opinion,—
that the course of events throughout the
world at the present time bears óut what
has just been said. One may draw the conclusion, that this is just the favorable moment to attempt to point out something,
which, in its true character, is foreign even
to those who are expert thinkers among
the parties and persons belonging to the
various schools of social thought. For it
may well be, that the tragedy that reveals
itself in all these attempts to solve the social question, arises precisely from the real
purport of the working-class struggle having been misunderstood,—misunderstood
even by those who, themselves with all
their opinions, are the outcome of this
struggle. For men by no means always
read their own purposes aright.

There may therefore seem some justification for putting these questions: What
is, in reality, the purport of the modern
working-class movement? What is its
will? Does this, its will and purport, cor-

respond to what is usually thought about it, either by the workers themselves, or by the non-workers? Does what is commonly thought about the "social problem" reveal that question in its *true form*? Or is an altogether different line of thought needed? This is a question which one cannot approach impartially unless, through personal destiny, one has in a position oneself to enter into the life of the modern worker's soul,—especially amongst that section of the workers who have most to do with the form the social movement is taking in the present day.

People have talked a great deal about the evolution of modern technical science and modern capitalism. They have studied the rise of the present working-class in the process of this evolution, and how the developments of economic life in recent times have led on to the workers' present demands. There is much that is to the point in what has been said about all this. But there is one critical feature which is never touched on, as one cannot help seeing, if one refuses to be hypnotised by the theory that it is external conditions that give the stamp to a man's life. It is a feature obvious to anyone who keeps an unclouded insight for impulses of the soul that work from within outwards, out of hidden depths. It is quite true, that the worker's demands have been evolved during the growth of modern technical science and modern capitalism; but a recognition of this fact affords no further clue whatever to the impulses that are actuating these demands, and which are in fact *purely human* in character. Nor, till one penetrates to the heart of these impulses, will one get to the true form of the social question.

There is a word in frequent use among the workers, which is of striking significance for anyone able to penetrate to the deeper-seated forces active in the human will. It is this: the modern worker has become *"class-conscious."* He no longer follows, more or less instinctively and unconsciously, the swing of the classes outside his own. He knows himself one of a class apart, and is determined, that the relation, which public life establishes between his class and the other classes, shall be turned to good account for his own interests. And anyone, who has comprehension for the undercurrents of men's souls, finds in the word "class-conscious," as used by the modern worker, a clue to very important facts in the worker's view of life,—in particular amongst those classes of workers, whose life is cast amidst modern technical industry and modern capitalism. What will above all arrest his attention is, how strongly the worker's soul has been impressed and fired by scientific teachings about economic life and its bearing on human destinies. Here one touches on a circumstance about which many people, who only think *about* the workers, not *with* them, have very hazy notions,—notions indeed, which are downright mischievous, in view of the serious events taking place at the present day. The view, that the "uneducated" working man

has had his head turned by Marxism, and
by later labour writers of the Marxist
school, and other things one hears of the
same sort, will not conduce towards that
understanding of the subject and its connection with the whole historic situation of
the world, which is so peculiarly necessary
at the present day. In expressing such a
view, one only shews that one lacks the will
to examine an essential feature of the present social movement. For it is an essential
feature, that the working-class consciousness has thus become filled with concepts
that take their stamp from the *scientific* evolution of recent times. This class-consciousness continues to be dominated by the note
struck in Lassalle's speech on "Science and
the Workers." Such things may appear
unessential to many a man who reckons
himself a "practical person"; but anyone,
who means to arrive at a really fruitful
insight into the modern labour movement-
is bound to turn his attention to these
things. In the demands put forward by
the workers to-day, be they moderates or

radicals, we have the expression, not, as many people imagine, of economic life that has—somehow—become metamorphosed into human impulse, we have the expression of e c o n o m i c s c i e n c e, by which the working-class consciousness is possessed. This stands out clearly in the literature of the labour movement, with its scientific flavour and popular journalistic renderings. To deny this, is to shut one's eyes to actual facts. And it is a fundamental fact, and one which determines the whole social situation at the present day, that everything which forms the subject of the worker's "class-consciousness" is couched for him in concepts of a scientific kind. The individual working at his machine may be no matter how completely a stranger to science; yet those, who enlighten him as to his own position and to whom he listens, borrow their method of enlightenment from this same science.

All the disquisitions about modern economic life, about the machine age and capitalism, may throw ever so instructive a

light on the facts underlying the modern
working-class movement; but the decisive
light on the present social situation does
not proceed directly from the fact, that the
worker has been placed at the machine,
that he has been harnessed to the capitalist scheme of things. It proceeds from the
other, different, fact, that his class-consciousness has been filled with a quite definite kind of *thought,* shaped at the machine and under the influence of the capitalist order of economy. Possibly the
habits of thought peculiar to the present
day may prevent many people from realising the full bearing of this circumstance,
and may cause them to regard the stress
laid upon it as a mere dialectic play upon
terms. One can only say in reply: So
much the worse for any prospect of a suc-
cessful intervention in social life to-day by
people who are unable to distinguish essentials. Anyone, who wants to understand the working-class movement, must
first and foremost know, how the worker
t h i n k s. For the working-class movement,

from its moderate efforts at reform to its
most sweeping extravagances, is not created by "forces outside man," by "economic impulses," but by h u m a n - b e i n g s, by
their mental conceptions and by the impulses of their will.

Not in what capitalism and the machine
have implanted in the worker's consciousness, not here lie the ideas and will-forces,
that give its character to the present social
movement.   This movement turned in the
direction of modern science to find its
fount of thought, because capitalism and
the machine could give the worker no substance with which to content his soul as a
human being.   Such substance and content
was afforded to the medieval craftsman
by his craft.   In the kind of connection
which the medieval handworker felt between himself, as a human being, and his
craft, there was something that shewed
life within the whole human confraternity
in a light which made it seem, for his individual consciousness, worth living.
Whatever he might be doing, he was able

to regard it in such a way, that he seemed through it to be realising what he desired, as a "man," to be. Tending a machine under the capitalist scheme of things the man was thrown back upon himself, upon his own inner life, whenever he tried to find some principle on which to base a general outlook on Man and one's consciousness of what as a "man" one is. Technical industry, capitalism,—these could contribute nothing towards such an outlook. And so it came to pass, that the working-class consciousness took the bent towards the scientific type of thought. The direct human link with actual life was lost.

Now this occurred just at a time, when the leading classes of mankind were working towards a scientific mode of thought, which in itself no longer possessed the spiritual energy to content man's consciousness in every aspect and guide it along all the directions of its wants. The old views of the universe gave man his place as a soul in the spiritual complex of existence. Modern science views him as a natural object amidst a purely natural order of things. This science is not felt as a stream flowing from a spiritual world into the soul of man, and on which man as a soul is buoyed and upborne. Whatever one's opinion may be as to the relation of the religious impulses, and kindred things, to the scientific mode of thought of recent times, yet one must admit, if one considers historic evolution impartially, that the scientific conception has developed out of the religious one. But the old conceptions of the universe, that rested deep down on religious foundations, lacked power to impart their soul-bearing force to the newer form of scientific conception. They withdrew beyond its range, and lived on, contenting their consciousness with things in which the souls of the workers could find no resource. For the leading classes, this inner world of consciousness might still have a certain value. In some form or other it was bound up with their own position in life. They sought for no new substance for their consciousness, because they were

able to keep a hold on the old one, that had
been handed down to them through actual
life.   But the modern worker was torn
out of all his old setting in life.   He was
the man whose life had been put on a totally new basis.   For him, when the old
bases of life were withdrawn, there dis-
appeared at the same time all possibility of
drawing from the old spiritual springs.
These lay far off in regions to which he
was now become a stranger.   Contemporaneous with modern technical science
and modern capitalism,—in such a sense as
one can speak of great worldstreams of
history as contemporaneous,—there grew
up the modern scientific conception of the
world.   To this the trust, the faith, of the
modern worker turned.   It was here he
sought the new substance that he needed
to content his inner consciousness.   But
the working-class and the leading classes
were differently situated with regard to
their scientific outlook.   The leading
classes felt no necessity for making the
scientific mode of conception into a gospel

of life, for the support of their souls. No matter how thoroughly they might have permeated themselves with the scientific conception of a natural order of things, in which a direct chain of causality leads up from the lowest animals to man, this mode of conception remained nevertheless a merely theoretic persuasion. It never stirred their feelings, and impelled them to take life through and through in a way befitting such a persuasion. Take naturalists such as Vogt and the popular writer, Buechner; they were unquestionably permeated with the scientific mode of conception; but, alongside this, there was something else at work in their souls which kept their lives interwoven with a whole complex of circumstances, such as can those whose only intelligible justification can be the belief in a spiritual order of the world. Putting aside all prejudice, let us just imagine, how differently the scientific outlook affects a man whose personal existence is anchored in such a complex, from the modern artisan, who, in the few even-

ing hours that he has free from work,
hears the labour leader get up and address
him in this fashion: "Science in our time
has cured men of believing that they have
their origin in a spiritual world. They have
learnt better, and know now, that in the
far ages, long ago, they climbed about on
trees like any vulgar monkey. Science has
taught them too, that they were all alike
in their origin, and that it was a purely
natural one." It was a science that turned
on such thoughts as these, which met the
worker when he was looking for a substance to fill his soul and give him a sense
of his own place as m a n in the life of the
universe. He took the scientific outlook
on the world in thorough earnest, and drew
from it his own practical conclusions for
life. The technical, capitalistic age laid
hold of him differently from a member of
the leading classes. The latter had his
place in an order of life, which still bore
the shape once given it by soul-sustaining
forces; it was all to his interest to fit the
acquisitions of the new age into this set-

ting. But the worker, in his soul, was torn
loose from this order of life. It was not
capable of giving him one emotion that
could illumine and fill his own life with
anything of human worth. There was one
thing only, which could give the worker
any sense of what a "man" is, one thing
only that seemed to have emerged from
the old order of life endowed with the
power that awakens faith, and that was—
scientific thought. It may arouse a smile
in some of those who read this, to be told
of the "scientific" character of the worker's conceptions. Let them smile, who can
only think of the scientific habit of mind as
something that is acquired by many years
of application on the benches of "educational institutes," and then contrast this
sort of "science" with what fills the mind
of the worker who has "never learnt anything." What is for him a smiling matter,
are facts of modern life on which the fate
of the future turns. And these facts shew,
that many a very learned man lives un-
scientifically, whereas the unlearned work-

er brings his whole view of life into line
with that scientific learning, of which very
likely nothing has fallen to his share. The
educated man has made a place for science,
—it has a pigeon-hole of its own in the re-
cesses of his soul. But he himself has his
place in a network of circumstances in actual life, and it is these which give the
direction to his feelings. His feeling is
not directed by his science. The worker,
through the very conditions of his life, is
led to bring his conception of existence into
unison with the *general tone* of this science.
He may be very far from what the other
classes call "scientific," yet his life's course
is charted by the scientific lines of conception. For the other classes, some religious
or aesthetic, some general spiritual principle is the determining basis;—for him,
Science is turned into the creed of life,—
even though often it may be science filtered
away to its last little shallows and driblets
of thought. Many a member of the "foremost" classes feels himself to be "enlight-
ened" in religion, a "free-thinker." No

doubt his scientific convictions influence his conceptions; but in his feelings still throb the forgotten remnants of a traditional creed of life. What the scientific type of thought has not brought down from the old order, is the consciousness of being, as a spiritual type, rooted in a spiritual world. This was a peculiarity of the modern scientific outlook, which presented no difficulty to a member of the leading classes. Life to him was filled by old traditions. For the worker it was otherwise; his new situation in life drove the old traditions from his soul. He took over from the ruling classes as heritage the scientific mode of thought, and made this the basis of his consciousness of the life and being of man. But this "spiritual possession," with which he filled his soul, knew nothing of its derivation from an actual life of the spirit. The only spiritual life, that the workers could take over from the ruling classes, was of a sort that denied its spiritual origin.

I well know, how these thoughts will

affect people outside as well as inside the working-class, who, believing themselves to have a thorough practical acquaintance with life, regard the view here expressed as quite remote from realities. The language of actual facts, as spoken by the whole state of the world to-day, will more and more prove this belief of theirs to be a delusion. For anyone able to look at these facts without prejudice, it will be plain, that a view of life, which never gets beyond their external aspect, becomes ultimately inaccessible to any conceptions save such as have lost all touch with facts. Ruling thought has clung on so long in this "practical" way to facts,—that the thoughts themselves have ended by bearing no resemblance whatever to the facts. The present world-catastrophe might have taught many people a lesson in this respect. What did they think it possible might happen? And what really did happen? Is it to be the same with their thoughts about social problems?

I know too, how someone who professes

working-class views will feel about what has been said, and can hear him saying: "Just like the rest of them! trying to shunt the real gist of the social question off on to lines that promise to be smooth for the bourgeois sort." With his creed, he does not see how fate has brought him into this working-class life, and how he is trying to find his way in it with a type of thought inherited from the ruling-classes. He *lives* as a working-man but he *thinks* as a bourgeois. The new age is making it necessary to learn not only a new way of life, but a new way of thought also. The scientific mode of conception can only become substantial and life-supporting, when it evolves, in its own fashion, a power to content the whole of human life in all its aspects, such as the old conceptions of life once evolved in their way.

This points the path for the discovery in its true form of one factor in the modern labour movement. And having travelled it to the end, the worker's soul utters this cry of conviction: "I am striving

after spiritual life.   Yet this spiritual life
is i d e o l o g y , is merely man's own reflection of what is going on in the world outside, it does not come to us from a spiritual
world of its own."   In the transition to the
new age, the old spiritual life had turned
to something which, for the working-class
sense of life, is ideology. If one wants to
understand the mood of soul amongst the
workers, as it finds vent in the social demands of the present day, one must be able
to grasp the full possible effects of the
theory that spiritual life is ideology.   It
may be retorted :   "What does the average
working-man know of any such theory?
it is only a will-o'-the-wisp in the brains
of their more or less educated leaders." But
anyone who says so is talking wide of life,
and his doings in actual life will be wide
of it too. He simply does not know, what
has been going on in the life of the working-
class during the last half century.   He
does not know the threads that are woven
from the theory, that spiritual life is ideology, to the demands and actions of the out-

and-out socialist, whom he thinks so "ig-
norant";—yes, and to the deeds too of
those who "hatch revolution" out of the
blind promptings of the life within them.

Herein lies the tragedy overshadowing
all our interpretations of the social demands of the day, that in so many circles
there is no sense of what is forcing its way
up to the surface out of the souls of the
great masses of mankind,—that people
cannot turn their eyes to what is actually
taking place in men's inner life.   The non-
worker listens with dismay to the worker
setting forth his demands; and this is what
he hears:—"Nothing short of communal-
ising the means of production will make it
possible for me to have a life worthy of a
human being."   But the non-worker is
unable to form the faintest conception, of
how his own class, in the transition from
the old age to the new, not only summoned
the worker to labour at means of production that were not his, but failed even to
give him anything to satisfy and sustain
his soul in his labour.   People, who see

and act wide of the mark in this way, may say:—"But, after all, the working-man only wants to better his position in life and put himself on a level with the upper classes; where do the needs of his soul come in?" The working-man himself may even declare:—"I am not asking the other classes for anything for my soul; all I want, is to prevent them exploiting me any longer. I mean to put an end to existing class destinctions." Talk of this kind does not touch the essence of the social question. It reveals nothing of its *true form*. For, had the working population inherited from the leading classes a genuine spiritual substance, then they would have had a different consciousness within their souls, one which would have voiced their social demands in quite a different fashion from the modern workers, who can see in the spiritual life, as they have received it, merely an ideology. The workers, as a class, are convinced of the ideologic character of spiritual life; but the conviction renders them more and more unhappy. They are not definitely conscious of this unhappiness in their souls, but they suffer acutely from it, and it far outweighs, in its significance for the social question to-day, all demands for an improvement in external conditions, —justifiable as these demands are too in their own way.

The ruling classes do not recognise, that they are themselves the authors of that attitude of mind, which now confronts them militant in the labour-world. And yet, they are the authors of it, inasmuch as, out of their own spiritual world, they failed to bequeath to the workers anything but what must seem to the workers "ideology."

What gives to the present social movement its essential stamp, is not the demand for a change of conditions in the life of one class of men,—although that is the natural sign of it. Rather, *it is the manner in which this demand is translated by this class from a thought-impulse into actual reality.* Consider the facts impartially from this point of view. One will find per-

sons who aim at keeping in touch with
labour tendencies in thought, smile at any
talk of a spiritual movement proposing to
contribute anything towards the solution
of the social question. They dismiss it
with a smile, as ideology, empty theory.
From thought, from the mere life of the
spirit, there is nothing, they feel certain,
to be contributed to the burning social
problems of the hour. And yet, when one
looks at the matter more closely, it is forced
upon one, that the very nerve, the very
root-impulse of the modern movement,—
especially as a working-class movement,—
does not lie in the things about which the
modern worker talks, but in *thoughts*. The
modern working-class movement has
sprung, as perhaps no other similar movement in the world before it, *out of
thoughts*. When studied more closely, it
shews this in a most marked degree. I
am not throwing this out as an apercu, the
result of long pondering over the social
movement. If I may venture to introduce
a personal remark I was for years lecturer

at a working-man's institute, giving instruction to working men in a wide variety of subjects; and I think that it taught me what is living and stirring in the soul of the modern proletarian worker. And from this starting point, I had occasion to go on, and follow up the tendencies at work in the various trades unions and different callings. I think I may say, that I am not approaching the subject merely from theoretical considerations, but am putting into words the results arrived at through actual living experience.

Anyone,—only, unfortunately, so few of the leading intellectuals are in this position,—but anyone, who has learnt to know the modern labour movement where it was carried on by the workers themselves, knows how remarkable a feature it is in it, and how fraught with significance, that a certain *trend of thought* has laid intense hold on the souls of large numbers of men. What makes it at the present moment hard to adopt any line as regards the social conundrums that present themselves, is that

there is so little possibility of an understanding between the different classes. It
is so hard for the middle-class to-day to
put themselves into the soul of the worker,
—so hard for them to understand how the
worker's still fresh, unexhausted intelligence opened to receive a work such as that
of Karl Marx,—which, in its whole mode
of conception, no matter how one regards
its substance, measures the requirements
of human thought by such a lofty standard.
One man may agree with Karl Marx's intellectual system,—another may refute it;
and the arguments on either side may appear equally good. In some points it was
revised, after the death of Marx and his
friend Engels, by those who came later and
saw social life under a different aspect
from these leaders. I am not proposing
to discuss the substance of the Marxian
system. It is not this that seems to me
the significant thing in the modern working-class movement. The thing that to me
seems significant above all others is, that
it should be a fact, that *the most powerful*

impulse at work in the labour world is a thought-system. One may go so far as to put it thus :—No practical movement, no movement that was altogether a movement of practical life, making the most matter-of-fact demands of every-day humanity, has ever before rested so almost entirely on a basis of thought alone, as the present working-class movement does. Indeed it is in a way the first movement of its kind to take up its stand entirely on a scientific basis. One must however see this fact in its proper light. If one considers every-thing that the modern worker has con-sciously to say about his own views and purposes and sentiments, it does not seem to one, from a deeper observation of life, to be by any means the thing of main im-portance. What impresses itself as of real importance is, that what in the other classes is an appendage of one single branch of the soul's life,—the *thought-basis,* from which life takes its tone,—has been made by pro-letarian feeling into the thing on which the whole man turns. What has thus be-

come an inward reality in the worker is,
however, a reality that he cannot acknowledge. He is deterred from acknowledging
it, because thought-life has been handed
down to him as ideology. He builds up
his life in reality upon thoughts; yet feels
thoughts to be unreal ideology. This is a
fact that one must clearly recognise in the
human evolution of recent years, together
with all that it involves,—otherwise it is
impossible to understand the worker's
views of life and the way those, who hold
these views, set about realising them in
practice.

From the picture drawn of the worker's
spiritual life in the preceding pages, it will
be clear that the main features of this
spiritual life must occupy the first place
in any description of the working-class social movement in its true form. For it is
essential to the worker's way of feeling
the causes of his unsatisfactory social condition and endeavoring to remove them,
that both the feeling and the endeavour
take the direction given them by his spirit-

ual life.   And yet, at present, he can only
reject with contempt or anger the notion,
that in the spiritual foundations of the
social movement there is something that
presents a remarkable driving force.   How
should he recognise in spiritual life a force
able to bear him along, when he is bound
to feel it as ideology?   One cannot look to
a spiritual life, that one feels as ideology,
to open up the way out of a social situation, which one has resolved to endure no
longer.   The scientific cast of his thought
has turned not only science, but religion,
art, morality, and right also for the modern
worker into so many constituent parts of
human ideology.   Behind these branches
of the spiritual life he sees nothing of
the workings of an actual reality, which
finds its way into his own existence, and
can contribute something to material life.
To him, these things are only the reflected
shine, or mirrored image of the material
life.   Whatever reflex influence they may
have on the shaping of this material life,—
whether roundabout, through the concep-

tions of men's brains, or through being taken up into the impulses of the will, yet, originally, they arise out of the material life itself as ideologic emanations from it. These of themselves can certainly yield nothing that will conduce to the removal of social difficulties. Only out of the sphere of material processes themselves can anything arise that will lead to the desired end.

Modern spiritual life has been passed on from the leading classes of mankind to the working population in a form which prevents the latter from being aware of the force that dwells in it. This fact above all must be understood, when considering what are the forces that can help towards the solution of the social question. Should it continue to exert its present influence, then mankind's spiritual life must see itself doomed to impotence before the social demands of our day and the time to come. Its impotence is in fact an article of faith with a large part of the working-class, and openly pressed in Marxism and similar creeds. "Modern economic life"—they say

—"has evolved out of its earlier forms the present capitalistic one. This evolutionary process has brought the workers into an unendurable situation as regards capital. But evolution will not stop here, it will go on, and kill capitalism through the forces at work in capitalism itself and from the death of capitalism will spring the emancipation of the workers." Later socialist thinkers have divested this creed of the fatalistic character it had assumed amongst a certain school of Marxists. But even so its essential feature remains, and shews itself in this way:—that it would *not* occur to anyone, who wishes to be a true socialist to-day, to say: "If we discover anywhere a life of the soul, having its rise in the forces of the age, rooted in a spiritual reality, and able to sustain the whole man,—then such a soul life as this could radiate the power needed as a motor-force for the social movement." The man of to-day, who is obliged to lead the life of a worker, can cherish no such expectation from the spiritual life of the day; and this it is which gives the key-note to his soul. He needs a spiritual life from which power can come, —power to give his soul the sense of his human worth. For when the capitalist economic order of recent times caught him up into its machinery, the man himself, with all the deepest needs of his soul, was driven for recourse to some such spiritual life. But the kind of spiritual life which the leading classes handed on to him as ideology left his soul void. Running through all the demands of the modern working-class, is this longing for some link with the spiritual life, other than the present form of society can give; and this is what gives the directing impetus in the social movement to-day. This fact however is one that is rightly understood neither outside nor inside the working-class. Those outside the working-class do not suffer from the ideologic cast of modern spiritual life, which is of their own making. Those who are inside the working-class do suffer; but the very ideologic character of their inherited spiritual life has robbed them of all belief in the power of spiritual possessions, as such, to sustain and support them. On a right insight into this fact depends the discovery of a path out of the maze of confusion into which social affairs have fallen. The path has been blocked by the social system that has arisen with the new form of industrial economy under the influence of the leading classes. The strength to open it must be achieved.

People's thoughts in this respect will undergo a complete change, when once they come really to feel the full weight of this fact: That, in a human community where spiritual life plays a merely ideologic role, common social life lacks one of the forces that can make and keep it a living organism. What ails the body social to-day, is impotence of the spiritual life. And the disease is aggravated by the reluctance to acknowledge its existence. Once the fact is acknowledged, there will then be a basis on which to develop the kind of thinking needed for the social movement.

At present, the worker thinks that he has struck a main force in his soul, when he talks about his "class-consciousness." But the truth is, that ever since he was caught up into the capitalist economic machine he has been searching for a spiritual life that could sustain his soul and give him a "human-consciousness,"—a consciousness of his worth as man,—which there is no possibility of developing with a spiritual life that is felt as ideology. This "human-consciousness—was what he was seeking. He could not find it; and so he replaced it with "class-consciousness born of the economic life. His eyes are rivetted upon the economic life alone, as though some overpowering suggestive influence held them there. And he no longer believes that elsewhere, in the spirit or in the soul, there can be anywhere a latent force capable of supplying the impulse for what is needed in the social movement. All he believes is, that the evolution of an economic life, devoid of spirit and of soul, can bring about the particular state of things,

which he himself feels to be the one worthy
of man. Thus he is driven to seek his
welfare in a transformation of economic
life alone. He has been forced to the conviction, that with the mere transformation
of economic life all those ills would dis-
appear, that have been brought on through
private enterprise, through the egoism of
the individual employer, and through the
individual employer's powerlessness to do
justice to the claims of human self-respect
in the employee. And so the modern worker was led on to believe, that the only welfare for the body social lay in converting
all private ownership of means of production into a communal concern, or into actual communal property. This conviction
is due to people's eyes having been removed,
as it were, from everything belonging to
soul and spirit, and fixed exclusively on
the purely economic process.

Hence all the paradox in the working-
class movement. The modern worker believes, that industrial economy, the economic life itself, will of necessity evolve all

that will ultimately give him his rights as
man. These rights of man in full are what
he is fighting for. And yet, in the heart
of the fight something different makes its
appearance,—something which never could
be an outcome of the economic life alone.
It is a significant thing, which speaks most
forcibly, that here, right at the centre of
the many forms which the social question
assumes under the needs of human life to-
day, there is something that seems, in men's
belief, to proceed out of economic life,
which, however, never could proceed from
economic life alone,—something, that lies
rather in the direct line of evolution; leading up through the old slave system,
through the serfdom of the feudal age, to
the modern proletariat of labour. The circulation of commodities, of money, the system of capital, property-ownership, the
land system, these may have taken no matter what form under modern life; but at
the heart of modern life something else has
taken place, never distinctly expressed, not
consciously felt even by the modern work-

er, but which is the fundamental force actuating all his social purpose. It is this:—
The modern capitalist system of economy recognises, at bottom, nothing but *commodities* within its own province. It understands the creation of commodity-values as a process in the body economic. And in the capitalistic processes of the modern age something has been turned into a commodity, which the worker feels must not and cannot be a commodity.

If it were only recognised what a fundamental force this is in the social movement amongst the modern workers: this loathing that the modern worker feels at being forced to barter his labour-power to the employer, as goods are bartered in the market.,—loathing at seeing his personal labour-power play part as a factor in the supply and demand of the labour-market, just as the goods in the market are subject to supply and demand. When once people become aware what this loathing of the "labour-commodity" means for the modern social movement, when once they

straightly and honestly recognise, that the
thing at work there is not even emphati-
cally and drastically enough expressed in
socialist doctrines,—then they will have
discovered the second of the two impulses
which are making the social question to-
day so urgent, one may indeed say so burning,—the first being that spiritual life that
is felt as an ideology.

In old days there were slaves. The en-
tire man was sold as a commodity. Rather
less of the man, but still a portion of the
human-being himself was incorporated in
the economic process by serfdom. To-day,
capitalism is the power, through which
still a remnant of the human-being,—his
labour-power,—is stamped with the character of a commodity. I am not saying,
that this fact has remained unnoticed. On
the contrary, it is a fact which in social
life to-day is recognised as a fundamental
one, and which is felt to be something that
plays a very important part in the modern
social movement. But people in studying
it keep their attention solely fixed on eco-

nomic life. They make the question of
the nature of a commodity solely an economic one. They look to economic life
itself for the forces that shall bring about
conditions, under which the worker shall
no longer feel that his labour-power is playing a part unworthy of him in the body
social. They see, how the modern form
of industrial economy came about historically in the recent evolution of mankind.
They see too, how it gave the commodity
character to human labour-power. What
they do not see, is, that it is a necessity inherent in economic life, that everything
incorporated in it becomes a commodity.
Economic life consists in the production
and useful consumption of commodities.
One cannot divest human labour-power of
its commodity character, unless one can
find a way of separating it out from the
economic process. It is of no use trying to
remodel the economic process so as to give
it a shape in which human labour may
come by its rights inside that process itself. What one must endeavor, is to find

a way of separating labour-power out from the economic process, and bringing it under *social* forces that will do away with its commodity character. The worker sets his desire upon some arrangement of economic life, where his labour-power shall find a fitting place; not seeing, that the commodity character of his labour is inherently and essentially due to his being bound up in the economic processes as part and parcel of them. Being obliged to surrender his labour-power to the economic processes, the whole man himself is caught up into them. So long as the economic system has the regulating of labour-power, it will go on consuming labour-power just as it consumes commodities,—in the manner that is most useful to its purposes. It is as though the power of economic life hypnotised people, so that they can look at nothing except what is going on inside it. They may look for ever in this direction without discovering how labour-power can escape being a commodity. Some other form of industrial economy will only make labour-power a commodity in some other manner. The *labour* question cannot find place in its true shape as part of the *social* question, until it is recognised that the considerations of economic life which determine the laws governing the circulation, exchange and consumption of commodities, are not such whose competence should be extended to human labour-power.

New age thought has not learned to distinguish the totally different fashions in which the two things enter into economic life: i. e., on the one hand, labour-power, which is intimately bound up with the human-being himself; and, on the other hand, those things that proceed from another source and are dissociated from the human-being, and which circulate along those paths that all commodities must take from their production to their consumption. Sound thinking on these lines will shew both the true form of the labour-power question, and the place that economic life must occupy in a healthily constituted society.

From this, it is obvious that the "social question" will divide itself into three distinct questions. The first is the question of a healthy form of spiritual life within the body social; the second, the consideration of the position of labour-power, and the right way to incorporate it in the life of the community. Thirdly, it will be possible to deduce the proper place and function of economic life.

II.

How Actual Life Requires that We Should Set about Solving Social Needs and Problems

The characteristic feature, then, to which the special form of the social question in recent times is directly traceable, may be expressed as follows: The modern life of industrial economy, grounded in technical science,—modern capitalism,—all this has acted in a sort of instinctive way, like a force of nature, and given modern social life its peculiar internal structure and method. But whilst men's attention grew thus absorbed in all that technical industry and capitalism brought with them, it became at the same time diverted from other branches, other departments of social life,—departments whose workings no less require direction by conscious human intelligence, if the body social is to be a healthy one.

I may perhaps be allowed to start by drawing a comparison, in order the better to describe what here, in any really comprehensive study of the social question, reveals itself as a powerful, indeed a main, actuating impulse. It must however be borne in mind, that this comparison is intended as a comparison only, used to help out the human understanding and give it the turn of thought needed for picturing what health in the body social implies. Accepting this point of view, then, if one turns to the study of that most complex of all natural organisms, the human organism, it is noticeable, that, running through the whole structure and life of it, there are three systems, working side by side, and each functioning to a certain extent separately and independently of the others. These three neighbor systems may be distinguished as follows: One system, forming a province all to itself in the natural human organism, is that which comprises the life of *the nerves and senses*. It may be named, after the principal part of the organism where the nerve and sense-life is more or less centred,—the h e a d - s y s t e m. Second comes what I should like to call t h e r h y t h m i c s y s t e m, which, to arrive at any real understanding of man's organisation, must be recognised as forming another branch to itself. This rhythmic system comprises the breathing, the circulation of the blood,—all that finds expression *in rhythmic processes* within the human organism. The third system, then, must be recognised as comprising all those organs and functions that have to do with actual matter-changes—the metabolic process. These three systems together comprise everything which, duly co-ordinated, keeps the whole human complex in healthy working order.

In my book, "Riddles of the Soul," I have already attempted to give a brief description of this threefold character of

the natural human organism in a way that
tallies completely with what scientific re-
search has as yet to tell us on the subject.
It seems to me clear, that biology, physiol-
ogy, and natural science in general as it
deals with man, are all rapidly tending to
a point of view which will shew, that what
keeps the whole complex process of the
human organism in working order is just
this comparatively separate functioning of
its three separate systems, the head system,
the circulation, or chest system and the
metabolic system,—that there is *no such
thing as absolute centralisation in the human organism,* and, moreover, that each
of these systems has its own special and
distinct relation to the outer world, the
head system through the senses, the rhythmic or circulatory system through the
breathing, the metabolic system through
the organs of nourishment and organs of
movement. What I have here indicated
goes much deeper down to spiritual sources
that I have tried to utilise for natural
science. In natural-science circles them-

selves, it is a fact not yet so generally recognised as might perhaps be desirable for the advancement of knowledge; but that merely means that our habits of thought, our whole way of picturing the world to ourselves, is not yet completely adapted to the inner life and being of nature's workings, as manifested, for instance, in the human organism. People of course may say, "No matter. Natural science can afford to wait. She will come to her ideals bit by bit, and views such as yours will gain recognition all in good time." But the body social cannot afford to wait, neither for the right views nor for the right practice. Here an understanding is necessary, —if only an instinctive one,—of what the body social needs,—and not merely an understanding amongst a handful of experts, but in every single human soul;—for every human soul takes its own share in the general working of the body social. Sane thinking and feeling, sane will and desires as to the form to be given the body social,— these are only to be developed, when one

comes to recognise,—even though only instinctively,—that, in order to thrive, the
social organism, like the natural one, requires to be threefold.

Now, since Schäffle wrote his book on
the structure of the social organism, all
sorts of attempts have been made to trace
out analogies between the organic structure of a natural creature,—a human being, say,—and of a community of human
beings. People have tried to map out the
body social into cells, network of cells, tis-
sues and so forth. Only a little while ago,
there was a book published by Merey,
"World Mutations," in which various natural science facts and laws were simply
transferred to what is supposed to be man's
social organism. That sort of analogy-
game has nothing whatever to do with
what is meant here; and anyone who mistakes what is said above for just such another play upon analogies between the natural and the social organism, has plainly
not entered into the spirit of these observa-
tions. The present comparison is not an

attempt to take some natural science truth and transplant it into the social system. Its object is quite different:—namely, to use the human body as an object lesson for training human thought and feeling to a sense of what organic life requires, and then to apply this perceptive sense to the body social. If one simply transfers to the body social something one thinks one has found out about the human body,— as is commonly done,—it merely shews that one is not willing to acquire the faculties needed for studying the social organism in the way one has to study the natural organism,—that is, as a thing by itself, with special laws of its own.

It might again be thought, that this manner of depicting the social organism arises from the belief that it should be "built up" after some cut-and-dried theory borrowed from natural science. Nothing could be further from all that is here in question. What I am trying to shew is something very different. The present crisis in the history of mankind demands the development in every single human being of certain faculties of apprehension, of which the first rudiments must be started by the schools and system of education,—like the first four rules of arithmetic. Hitherto, the body social received its older forms from something that never entered consciously into the life of the human soul; but in the future this force will cease to be active. Fresh evolutionary impulses are coming in, and from now on will be active in human life; and it is part of them, that every individual should be required to have these faculties of apprehension, just as each individual has long been required to have a certain measure of education. From now on, it is necessary that the individual should be trained to have a healthy sense of how the forces of the body social must work in order for it to live. People must learn to feel, that it would be unhealthy, anti-social, *n o t* to possess such sense of what the body social needs and to want to take one's place in it.

One hears much talk to-day about "socialisation" as the thing that the age needs. But this socialisation will prove no true cure but a quack remedy, possibly even a fatal one for social life, unless in men's hearts, in men's souls, there dawns at least an *instinctive* perception of the necessity for a *threefold division of the body social.* If the body social is to function healthily, it must regularly develope three organic divisions such as here described.

One of these three divisions is the e c o - n o m i c l i f e . It is the best one to begin with here, because it has obviously, through modern technical industry and modern capitalism, worked its way into the whole structure of human society, to the subordination of everything else. This economic life requires to form an independent organic branch by itself within the body social,—relatively as independent as the nervous and sensory system within the human body. Its concern is with everything in the nature of production of commodities, circulation of commodities, consumption of commodities.

Next comes the life of p u b l i c r i g h t,
—political life in the proper sense. This
must be recognised as forming a second
branch of the body social. To this branch
belongs what one might term the true life
of the State,—taking "State" in the sense
in which it was formerly applied to a community possessing common rights.

Whilst economic life is concerned with
all that a man needs from Nature and what
he himself produces from nature,—with
commodities and the circulation and consumption of commodities,—the second
branch of the body social can have no other
concern than what is involved in purely
human relations, in that which comes up
from the deep-recesses of the inner life
and affects man's relation towards man.
It is essential to a right understanding of
the composition of the social organism, that
one should clearly recognise the difference
between the system of *"public right,"*
which can only deal from inner and purely
human grounds with man-to-man relations,
and the *economic system,* which is concerned

solely with the production, circulation and consumption of commodities. People must become possessed of an instinctive sense for distinguishing between these two in life, so that in practice the economic life and the life of "right" will be kept distinct;—just as, in man's natural organism, the lungs' fuction in working up the outer air keeps distinct from the processes going on in the nervous and sensory life.

As the *third* division, alongside the other two and equally independent, are to be understood all those things in the social organism which are connected with mental and spiritual life. The term "spiritual culture," or "everything that is connected with mental and spiritual life," is scarcely a term that accurately describes it in any way. Perhaps one might more accurately express it as "Everything that rests on the natural endowments of each single human being—everything that plays a part in the body social on the ground of the natural endowments, both spiritual and physical, of the individual."

The first function,—the economic one,— has to do with everything that must exist in order that man may keep straight in his material adjustments to the world around him. The second function has to do with whatever must exist in the body social because of men's personal relations to one another. The third function has to do with all that must spring from the personal individuality of each human being, and must be incorporated as personal individuality in the body social.

The more true it is that our social life has of recent years taken its stamp from modern technical industry and modern capitalism, the more necessary it is, that the injury thus unavoidably done to the body social should be healed by bringing man, and man's communal life, into right relation to these three systems of the body social. Economic life has, in recent times, singly and of itself, taken on quite new forms. And because it has worked all alone, unbalanced, it has asserted undue power and preponderance in human life.

The two other branches of social life have not until now been in a position to work themselves in this matter-of-course way into the social organism and become incorporated with it according to their own proper laws. Here man must step in, with the instinctive sense I spoke of, and set to work to evolve the threefold order, each individual working *on* the spot and *at* the spot where he happens to be. To attempt to solve the social problem in the way meant here, will leave not one individual without his task, now and in the days that are coming.

To begin with the first division of the body social, the e c o n o m i c l i f e:—This is grounded primarily in conditions of Nature,—just as the individual man starts with special qualities of mind and body as the basis for what he may be able to make of himself by study, education and the teaching of life. This nature-basis sets a unique stamp on economic life, and through economic life on the whole organism of society. It is *there,* this nature-basis, and no methods of social organisation, no manner of socialising measures, can affect it,—at least, not radically. One must accept this nature-basis as the groundwork of life for the body social,—just as, in educating an individual, one must take his natural qualities as groundwork,—how nature has endowed him in this or that respect, his mental and physical power. Every experiment in socialisation, every attempt at giving man's communal life an economic form, must take this nature-basis into account. At the bottom of all circulation of commodities, of all human labour, and of every form of spiritual life too, there lies something primal, elementary, basic, which links man to a bit of nature. The connection between a social organism and its nature-basis is a thing that has to be taken into consideration,—just as one has to consider an individual in regard to his personal endowment, when it is a question of his learning something.—This is most obvious in extreme cases. Take, for instance, those parts of the earth, where the banana affords man an easily accessible form of food. Here, it will be a question of the amount and kind of labour that must be expended to bring the banana from its place of origin to a convenient spot and deliver it ready for consumption; and this will enter into all considerations of men's communal life together. If one compares the human labour, that must be exerted to make the banana ready for human consumption, with the labour that must be exerted in Central Europe, say, to make wheat ready for consumption, it is at least three hundred times less for the banana than for the wheat.

Of course that is an extreme case. But similar differences in proportion to the nature-basis exist between the amounts of labour that are requisite in the other branches of production represented in the various social communities of Europe. The differences are not so marked as in the case of bananas and wheat,—still, they exist. Accordingly, it is inherent to the body economic, that the amount of labour-

power which man has to put into the economic process is proportionate to the nature-basis of his economic activities. Com-
pare the wheat-yields alone:—In Germany,
in districts of average fertility, the returns
on wheat cultivation represent about a
sevenfold to eightfold crop on the seed
sewn; in Chile, the crop is twelvefold; in
Northern Mexico, seventeenfold; in Peru,
twentyfold.   (See *Jensen*.)

The whole of this living complex of
processes, that begin with man's relation
to nature, and continue through all that
man has to do to transform nature's products, down to the point where they are
ready for consumption,—these processes,
and these alone for a healthy social organism, comprise its economic system.   In the
social organism, the economic system occupies somewhat the same place as is occupied in the whole human organism by
the head-system, which conditions the individual's abilities.   But this head-system
is dependent on the lung-and-heart system;
and in the same way the economic system

is dependent on the services of human labour. The head, however, cannot of itself alone regulate the breathing; and neither should the system of human labour-power be regulated by the forces that are operative within the economic life itself. It is through his interests that man is engaged in economic life, and these have their foundation in the needs of his soul and spirit.—In what way can a social organism most expediently incorporate men's interests, so that on the one hand the individual may find in this social organism the best possible means of satisfying his personal interest, whilst being economically employed to the best advantage?—This is the question that has to be practically solved in the institutions of the body economic. It can only be solved, if these individual interests are given really free scope, and if at the same time there exists the will and possibility to do what is necessary to their satisfaction. These interests arise in a region outside the confines of the economic life. They grow up as man's own being unfolds its soul and physical nature. It is the business of economic life to make arrangements for their satisfaction. The only arrangement however that the economic life can make, are such as are limited to the delivery and exchange of commodities,—that is of goods which acquire their value from men's wants. The value of a commodity comes from the person consuming it. And owing to the fact, that its value comes from the consumer, a commodity occupies quite a different position within the social organism from other things that have a value for man as part of that organism. Study the whole circle of economic life, putting aside all preconceptions,—the production, circulation and consumption of commodities going on within it. One observes at once the difference *in character* between the relation that arises when one man makes commodities for another, and that human relation that has its foundation in mutual right. One will not however stop short at merely observing the difference; one will follow it up practically, and insist that economic life and the life of "right" should be kept completely separate within the body social. Institutions devoted to the production and exchange of commodities require men to develope forms of activity that are not immediately productive of the very best impulses for their mutual relations in "right." Within the economic sphere man turns to his fellow because it suits their reciprocal interests. Radically different is the link between man and man in the sphere of "right."

It may be thought perhaps, that the distinction which life requires between the two things is adequately recognised, if the institutions established for the purposes of economic life also make provision for the "rights" that are involved in the mutual relations of the people engaged in it. But such a notion has no root in reality. The relation "in right," that necessarily exists between a man and his fellows, is one that can only be rightly felt and lived *outside* the economic sphere, on totally dif-

ferent soil, not *inside* it. In the healthy
social organism, therefore, there must be
another system of life, alongside the economic life and independent of it, where
human rights can grow up and find suitable administration. But the "rights" life
is, strictly, the political sphere,—the true
sphere of the State. If the interests that
men have to serve in their economic life
are carried over into the legislation and
administration of the "rights" State, then
these rights as they grow up will merely
be an expression of economic interests;
whilst, if the "rights" State takes on the
management of economic affairs, it is no
longer fitted to rule men's "life of rights";
since all its measures and institutions will
be forced to serve man's need for commodities, and thereby diverted from those
impulses which make for the life of rights.

A healthy social organism, therefore, requires, as a second branch alongside the
body economic, the independent political
life of the State. In the separate body economic, the forces of economic life itself

will guide men to such institutions as best
serve the production and interchange of
commodities. In the body politic, the State,
institutions will arise, where dealings between individuals and groups will be settled on lines that satisfy men's sense of
right. This demand for complete separation of the "rights-State" from the economic sphere proceeds from a standpoint
of reality. Reality is not the standpoint of
those who seek to combine the life of rights
and economics in one. The people engaged
in economic life of course possess the sense
of right, but they will only be able to legis-
late and administrate in the way "right"
requires,—i. e., from the sense of right
alone without any admixture of economic
interests,—when they come to consider
questions of right independently, in a
"rights" State that takes, quâ State, no part
in economic life. A "rights" State, such
as this, has its own legislative and administrative bodies, both constructed according to those principles that ensue from the
modern sense of right. It will be built up

on those impulses in human consciousness, which go to-day by the name of "democratic." The legislative and administrative bodies in the economic domain will arise out of the forces of economic life. Such transactions as are necessary between the *executive heads* of the legislative and administrative bodies of "rights" and economics respectively, will be carried on pretty much as between the governments of sovereign states to-day. This co-ordination of the two systems will make it possible for developments in the one body to exert the needful influence on the other. This influence of the two spheres on one another is prevented, when one of them tries to develope within itself the element that should come to it from the other.

The economic life, then, is dependent on the one hand on those relations in "right," which the State establishes between the persons and groups of persons engaged in economic work, just as, on the other hand, it is subject to the conditions of the nature-basis (climate, local fea-

tures, presence of mineral wealth, etc.).
The bounds are thus marked out on either
side for the proper and possible activities
of economic life.   Just as nature creates
predetermining conditions, which lie outside the economic sphere, and must be ac-
cepted by the man at work in it as the
given premises on which all his economic
work must be based,—so everything in the
economic sphere that establishes a "relation in right" between man and man, must,
in a healthy social organism, be regulated
by the "rights-State," which, like the nature-basis, goes on alongside and independently of the economic life.   In the
present social organism,—as developed in
the course of mankind's historic evolution
up till now,—economic life occupies an un-
duly large place, and sets the peculiar
stamp that it has acquired from the ma-
chine-age and modern capitalism upon the
whole social movement.   It has come to include more than it should include in any
healthy society.   In the present day, traf-
ficking to and fro within the economic cir-

cuit, where only *commodities* should traffic, we find *human labour-power,* and *human rights* besides. At the present day, within the body economic, one can truck not only commodities for commodities, but commodities for human labour,—and for human rights as well, and all by the very same economic process. (By "c o m m o d i t y" I mean everything which through human activity has acquired the form in which it is finally brought by man to its place of destination for consumption. Economists may perhaps find this definition objectionable or inadequate; but it may be serviceable towards an understanding of what properly belongs to economic life.§§)

When anyone acquires a plot of land by purchase, one must regard it as an exchange of the land for commodities for

---

(§§). *Author's Note.* For the purposes of life, what is wanted in an explanation is not definitions drawn from theory, but ideas that give a picture of a real live process. As used in this sense, *"commodity"* denotes something that plays an actual part in man's life and experience, Any other concept of it either omits or adds to this, and so fails to tally exactly with what really and truly goes on in life.

which the purchase money stands proxy. The plot of land however does not act as a commodity in economic life. It holds its position in the body social through the *"right"* the owner has to use it. There is an essential difference between this *right* of use, and the relation of a producer to the commodity he produces. From the very nature of the producer's relation to his product, it cannot possibly enter into the totally different kind of man-to-man relation created by the fact that someone has been granted the sole right to use a certain piece of land. Other men are obliged to live on this land, or the owner sets them to work on it for their living; and thus he brings them into a State of dependence upon himself. The fact of mutually exchanging genuine commodities, which one produces or consumes, does not establish a dependence that affects the man-to-man relation in the same kind of way.

To an unprejudiced mind it is clear, that a fact of actual life, such as this, must, in a healthy society, find due expression in its social institutions. So long as there is simply an interchange of commodities for commodities in economic life, the value of these commodities is determined independently of the relations-of-right existing between individuals or groups. Directly commodities are interchanged for rights, the "rights relation" is itself affected. It is not a question of the exchange in itself; such an exchange is the inevitable life-element of the modern social organism, resting as it does on division of labour. The point is, that through this interchange of rights and commodities, "right" itself is turned into a commodity, when the source of "right" lies within the economic life. The only way of preventing this, is by having two sets of institutions in the body social,—one, whose sole and only object it is to conduct commodities in the most expedient manner along its circuit, the other regulating those human rights involved in commodity-exchange which arise between the individuals engaged in producing, trading and consuming. Such rights are not distinct in their nature from any other rights that necessarily exist in all relations between persons, quite independent of commodity-exchange. If I injure or benefit my fellow-man by the sale of a commodity, it falls within the same social category as an injury or benefit due to some action or negligence not directly expressed in an exchange of commodities.

In the organisation of economic life, that familiarity with business, which comes from practical experience and specialist training, will give the point of view needed by the person at the head of affairs. In the "rights" organisation, the laws and administration will give effect to the general sense of right in the dealings of persons and groups with one another. The economic organisation will assist the formation of Associations amongst people who from their calling, or as consumers, have the same interests or similar requirements. And this network of Associations, working together, will build up the whole fabric of industrial economy. The economic organisation will grow up on an associative basis, and out of the links between the Associations. The work of the Associations will be purely economic in character, and be carried on on a basis of "rights" provided by the rights-organisation. These Associations, being able to make their economic interests recognised in the representative and administrative bodies of the economic organisation, will not feel any need to force themselves into the legislative or executive government of the "rights-State" (as, for instance, a Landowners' League, or Manufacturers' Party, or a Socialist party representing an industrial programme), in order to effect there what they have no power to achieve within the limits of the economic life. If the "rights-State" again takes no part whatever in any branch of industrial economy, then the institutions it establishes will be such only as spring from the sense of right amongst its members. Although the persons who sit on the representative body of the rights-State may, and of course will, be the same as are taking an active part in economic life, yet, owing to the division of function, economic life will not be able to exert such an influence on the "rights life," that the health of the whole body social is undermined,—as it can be, when the state itself organises branches of economic life, with representatives of the economic world as state-legislators, making laws to suit economic interests.

A typical example of the fusion of the economic life with the rights-life was afforded by Austria. According to the constitution adopted by Austria in the eighteen-sixties, the representatives of the imperial assembly, the "Reichsrat," of that compound territory, were elected from the communities representing the four branches of economic life:—the landed .proprietors,—the chambers of commerce, —the towns, markets and industrial centres,—and the rural areas. Obviously, in this composition of the representative State-assembly, the first and only idea was, that of playing off the economic interests

against one another, in the belief that a
system of political rights must be the outcome.   No doubt the disruptive forces of
her divers nationalities contributed largely
to Austria's downfall.   But it may be taken
as no less certain, that if an opportunity
had been given for developing a system of
"rights," working alongside and outside of
the economic one, it would, from the common sense of right, have evolved a form
of society in which the different nationalities could have lived together in unity.

A person engaged in public life to-day
usually turns his attention to things in it
that are only of secondary consideration.
This is because his habits of thought lead
him to regard the body social as uniform
in structure.   As a uniform structure,
there is no form of suffrage he can devise
that will fit it; for the economic interest
and the impulses of human rights will come
into mutual conflict upon the representative body, however it may be elected; and
the conflict between them will affect social
life in a way that must result in severe

shocks to the whole organism of society. The first and indispensable object to be worked for in public life to-day must be the radical separation of economic life from the "rights" organisation. And as the separation becomes gradually established, and people grow into it, the two organisations will each in the process discover its own most appropriate method of selecting its legislators and administrature. Amongst all that at the present moment is clamouring for settlement, forms of suffrage, although they bear on fundamental issues, are nevertheless of secondary consideration.

Where the old conditions still exist, these can be taken as the basis from which to work towards the new separation of function. Where the old order has already melted away, or is in process of dissolution, there individuals and little groups of people must find the initiative to start reconstructing along the new lines of growth. To try in 24 hours to effect a transformation in public life, is recognised by thoughtful socialists themselves as midsummer madness. They look to gradual opportune changes to bring about what they regard as social welfare. The light of facts, how- ever,—must make it plain to any impartial observer, that a reasoning will and purpose are needed to make a new social order, and are imperatively demanded by the forces at work in mankind's historic evolution.

These remarks will be regarded as "un- practical" by someone who regards noth- ing as practicable outside the narrow hori- zon of his customary life. Unless he can see things differently, any influence he may retain in any sphere of life will not tend to heal the disease in the body social, but only to make it worse. It was people of his way of thinking who helped to bring about the present state of affairs. There must be a reversal of the movement which has set in in leading circles, and which has already brought various departments of economic life (e. g., the postal and railway services, etc.), within the workings of the State. Its opposite must begin: a movement towards the elimination of all economic activity from the domain of politics and State organisation. Thinkers, whose whole will and purpose, as they believe, is directed to the welfare of society, take this movement towards State control, started by the hitherto governing circles, and push it to its logical extreme. They propose to socialise all the materials of economic life, in so far as they are means of production. A healthy course of development, however, will give economic life its independence, and will give the political State a system of "right" through which it can bring its influence to bear on the body economic,— so that the individual shall not feel that his function within the body social gives the lie to his sense of right.

When one considers the work that a man does for the body social by means of his physical labour-power, it is plain that the above reflections are grounded in the actual life of men. The position which labour has come to occupy in the social order under the capitalistic form of economy, is such, that is purchased by the employer from the employed as a *commodity*. An exchange is effected between money (as representing commodities) and labour. But in reality no such exchange can take place; it only *appears* to do so. (§) What really happens is, that the employer receives in return from the worker commodities that cannot exist, unless the worker devotes his labour-power to creating them. The worker receives one part, the employer the other part of the commodity so created. The production of the commodity is the result of a co-operation between employer and employed. The product of their joint action is that which first passes into the circuit of economic life. For the product to come into existence, there must be a "relation in right" between worker and

---

(§). *Author's note.* It is quite possible in life for a transaction not only to be interpreted unreally, but also to take place unreally. *Money and labour are not interchangeable values,* but only money and the products of labour. Accordingly, if I give money for labour, *I am doing* something that is unreal. I am making a sham transaction. For in reality I can only give money for the product of labour.

"enterpriser"; but the capitalist type of
economy is able to convert this "rights"
relation into one determined by the employer's superiority in economic power
over the employed. In a healthy social
order, it will be obvious that labour cannot
be paid for, that one cannot set an economic value upon it comparable to the
value of a commodity. The commodity
produced by this labour first acquires an
economic value by comparison with other
commodities. The kind of work a man
must do for the maintenance of the body
social, how he does it, and the amount,
must be settled according to his abilities
and the conditions of a decent human existence. And this is only possible when such
questions are settled by the political state,
quite independently of the provisions and
regulations made in the economic life.

This settlement of labour conditions outside economics, pre-establishes a basis of
value for commodities comparable to the
basis already established by the conditions
of nature. The value of one commodity, as

measured by another, is increased by the
fact that its raw material is more difficult
to procure; and, similarly, the value of a
commodity must be made dependent on the
kind and amount of labour which the
"rights" system allows to be expended on
its production. (§§)

Thus economic life has its conditions
fixed on two sides. On one, there is the
"nature-basis," which man must take as
he finds it; on the other, will be the "rights-
basis" which has to be created on the free
and independent ground of the political
State,—detached from economic life, and
out of the common sense of right.

It is obvious, that in a social organism
conducted in this way the standard of economic well-being will rise and fall with the
amount of labour which the common sense

(§§). *Author's Note.* The "rights of the matter" becomes the axiomatic basis for all economic activity
under this relation of labour to the "rights" system;
and the associations will have to accept these as a given
premise in economic life. What this does, however,
is to make economic organisation dependent upon man,
instead of man being dependent upon the system of
economics.

of right expends upon it. This however must be so in a healthy society. Only the subordination of the general economic prosperity to the common sense of right can prevent man from being so used up and consumed by economic life that his existence no longer seems to him worthy of his humanity. And it is this sense of an existence unworthy of human beings that is, in reality, at the bottom of the convulsions in the body social.

Should the general standard of economic well-being be too greatly lowered on the "rights" side, there is a way of preventing this, just as there is a way of improving the nature-basis. One can employ technical means to make a less productive soil more productive; and, if prosperity declines over much, the mode and amount of work can be changed. Only, such changes should not be a direct consequence of processes in the economic life; they must be the outcome of *insight,* arrived at on the free ground of "rights," independent of economic life.

There is, however, another element again, which enters into everything that is contributed towards the organisation of social life, whether by the economic life or by the "rights-consciousness." This element comes from a third source: the personal abilities of the individual. This third domain includes everything from the loftiest achievements of the human mind to that element in all the works of men which comes from their bodily ability to render greater or less service to the body social. A healthy social organism must necessarily receive and assimilate whatever comes from this source in quite a different manner from what comes to it from the life of the State or that finds expression in the interchange of commodities. To absorb this element healthily into social life can only be done in one way, and that is, by leaving it entirely to men's free receptivity and to the impulses which personal ability itself brings with it. What is performed at the promptings of personal ability, loses to a great extent the very ground-

work of its existence, when subjected to
artificial influences from the State organisation or from the economic system.   For
the only true groundwork of such performances lies in that inherent force that
finds its evolution through human per-
formance itself.   If again the way in which
such individual performances are taken up
into the body social directly depends on
the economic life,—or if the State organises
it,—there is then a check upon that free
spontaneous receptivity, which is the only
sound and wholesome channel for their
reception.   For the spiritual life of the
body social, there is but one possible line
of healthy evolution;—and it must not be
forgotten, by what innumerable fine
threads this spiritual life is connected with
the evolution of all other individual poten-
tialities in human life.   What it does, must
be the outcome of its own impulses; and
those who receive its services must be
closely bound up with it in sympathy and
understanding.   Such, as here sketched,
are the requisite conditions for a sound

evolution of the spiritual life of the body
social. What prevents them from being
clearly perceived, is that people's eyes are
blurred through constantly seeing the spiritual life in great part fused and con-
founded with the political State system.
The fusion has been taking place through
several hundreds of years, and they have
grown accustomed to it. They talk, it is
true, about "freedom of knowledge" and
"freedom of education"; but, all the same,
they consider it a matter of course that the
political State should have control of this
"free" knowledge and "free" education.
They do not see nor feel, how in this way
the state is bringing all spiritual life into
dependence on state requirements. The notion is, that the State provides the educational posts, and that the spiritual life then
unfolds "freely" under the hands of the
people who fill these State posts. Through
long thinking in this way, people come to
forget what an intimate connection there
is between the inmost nature of man and
the *substance* of the spiritual life growing

up within him, and how impossible it is
for the growth of this spiritual substance
to be really free, if it owes its place in the
body social to any other impulses than
those alone which proceed from the spiritual life itself. Science, with all that part
of spiritual life which it affects, has received its whole cast from the fact of its
management forming part of the State system in recent centuries. And not only so,
but this fusion with the State has set its
stamp on the *substance* of science as well.
Of course, the results of mathematics or
physics cannot be directly influenced by
the State. But consider history and other
subjects of general culture:—Have not
they come to reflect the connection of their
professional representatives with the State
system?—to be an obedient mirror of State
requirements?

The peculiar stamp thus acquired by our
present-day mental conceptions, in which
the scientific turn of thought predominates
over every other, is just what makes them
a mere ideology as they affect the working-

class. The workers have observed, how men's thoughts acquire a certain character, arising out of the requirements of state life,—a State life that suits the interests of the ruling classes. It was a reflection of material interests, and of the war of interests, that the worker saw when he looked into his thoughts. Thus there arose in him a sense that all spiritual life whatever was ideology, a mirrored image of the economic order of affairs. Such a view of things works havoc with men's spiritual life. But its blighting effects will cease, once it becomes possible for them to feel that in the spiritual domain there reigns a reality that transcends material outward life and bears its own substance within itself. No such sense of a spiritual reality can, however, possibly arise, unless the spiritual life is free within the body social to expand and govern itself according to the impulses inherent in it. Only those, who have their part in a spiritual life thus freely expanding and freely governed, can represent it with that strength and vigour which shall ensure it its due place within the body social. Such an independent position within human society is indispensable for art, science and a philosophy of life, with all that goes with these. The freedom of one cannot prosper without the freedom of all. Although in their substance mathematics and physics may not be influenced directly by State requirements, yet how they are applied, the estimate people form of their value, the effect their pursuit has upon the rest of spiritual life, all these and many other points are determined by State requirements, whenever some of the branches of spiritual life are under State control. It is one thing, when the teacher of the lowest grade in the school follows the line along which the State impells him; it is another, when he takes his line from a spiritual life that rests on its own independent footing. Here again, social democracy has done no more than take over a habit of thought and conventions inherited from the ruling classes. Social democracy

sets before itself as an ideal the incorpora-
tion of spiritual life in a social structure
based on a system of industrial economy.
But, were its aim attained, it would be only
a further step along the same road that has
led to the present depreciation of spiritual
life.   It was a right feeling, but a one-
sided one that found expression in the socialist maxim: "Religion is a man's private affair"; for, in a healthy society, *all*
spiritual life must in this sense be a private affair, so far as concerns the State and
economic life.   Only, social democracy does
not relegate religion to the sphere of private affairs with any idea of thus establishing its status as spiritual wealth, and giving it a position within the social order
where it may attain to a higher and more
worthy development than under the State's
influence.   No; it's idea in so doing is, that
the resources of the body social should only
be used to cultivate what it needs for its
own existence, and that the religious kind
of spiritual wealth does not come under
this head.   This is not the way in which

one branch of spiritual life can prosper,
singled out as an exemption from public
life, whilst all the rest remain in bondage.
The religious life of mankind in this new
age will go hand in hand with emancipated
spiritual life in every form, and grow to a
force able to bear up the souls of the men
of the new age.

It is a matter for the soul's own free
demand, how the spiritual life is received
into men, no less than how it comes forth
from them. Teachers, artists and others
will find, that they have an altogether different influence, and are able to awaken an
understanding amongst the public for what
they are creating, when they themselves
have a place in the social order which has
no direct connection with any legislature
or government, but only with such as arise
from impulses that lie in the course of the
spiritual life itself; when too they are ap-
pealing to people, who are not simply under
compulsion to labour, but for whom an
autonomous and independent political State
also ensures the right to *leisure,*—leisure

which awakens the mind to an appreciation
of spiritual *values*.   Here one will very
likely be told by someone, that his own
"practical experience,"—of which he has
a great opinion,—convinces him, that if
this notion were carried out,—if the State
made definite provision for leisure hours,
and if school attendance were left to people's own sense, it would simply mean that
people would spend all their leisure in the
public house and relapse into a state of
brute ignorance.   Well, let such "pessi-
mists" wait and see what will happen when
the world is no longer under their influence.   Their line of action is all too often
prescribed by a subtle feeling, a secret
voice, that whispers in their ear, how they
themselves like to spend their leisure hours,
and the steps that were necessary to ensure
themselves having a decent education. Of
the free spiritual life, of its power to fire
and kindle, when left to itself within the
body social,—of this such persons naturally take no account.   They know the spiritual life in bondage only, and so it has no

power to kindle any spark within themselves.

Both the political State and the economic
system will obtain from the body spiritual,
when under its own self-administration,
that steady inflow from the spiritual life,
of which they are in need.   Practical training too for economic life will for the first
time fully develope its full possibilities,
when the economic system and the body
spiritual can co-operate in freedom.   People will come with a suitable training into
the economic field and will put life into all
they meet with there, through the strength
that comes from spiritual endowment set
free from restraint.   And people, who have
won their experience in the economic field,
will find their way into the spiritual organisation, and help to fertilise what there
needs fertilising.

The effect within the political State of
spiritual abilities being left free, will be
the growth of sane and sound views, such
as are needed in this field.   The man who
works with his hands will be able to feel

contented with the place his own labour
fills in the body social. He will come to
realise that the body social cannot float
him, unless his hand-work has the guidance
requisite for its organisation. He will
acquire a sense of the solidarity of his
own labour with those organising forces
which he can trace to the development of
personal talent. The political State will
afford him a ground on which he can establish the "rights" that secure to him his
share in the proceeds of the commodities
he produces; and he will freely allot to the
spiritual property, from which he benefits,
a portion sufficient to keep it productive.
There will be a possibility for producers
in the spiritual field, too, to live on the proceeds of their work. What anyone chooses
to do in the matter of spiritual work, will
be nobody's affair but his own; but for
any service he may render to the body social he will be able to count on willing
recompense from people to whom spiritual
goods are a necessity. Anyone, who is not
satisfied with the recompense he receives

under the spiritual organisation, must have recourse to one of the other fields, either to the political state, or to economic life.

Into the economic life pass those technical ideas which originate in the spiritual life. Their origin is in the spiritual life, even although they proceed directly from persons belonging to the State or to the economic world. In the spiritual life originate all those ideas and organising capacities that enrich the life of the State and of industrial economy. For everything thus supplied to both these fields of social life from the spiritual source, the recompense will either, as in the other cases, be raised through voluntary recognition on the part of those who directly draw from this source, or else it will be regulated by the "rights" that gradually become built up in the political sphere. What the political State itself needs for its own maintenance, will be raised by a system of taxation, which will be the outcome of a harmonious co-ordination of the claims of economic life, on the one hand, and those of the "rights-consciousness" on the other.

Alongside the political sphere and the economic sphere in a healthy society, there must be the spiritual sphere, functioning independently on its own footing. The whole trend of the evolutionary force of modern mankind is in the direction of this threefolding of the social organism. So long as the life of the community could be guided in all essentials by the instinctive forces at work in the mass of mankind, so long there was no urgent tendency towards this definite separation into three functions. At bottom, there were always these three distinct sources; but in a yet dim and dully conscious social life they worked together as one. Our modern age demands conscious co-operation on the part of man, and that he should take his place open-eyed in the workings of the body social. This new social consciousness must, however, be directed from three aspects, if it is to shape men's life and conduct healthily. It is this threefold line of evolution towards which modern humanity is striving in the soul's unconscious depths; and what finds outlet in the social movement is but the stormy light cast up from the fires below.

At the end of the eighteenth century, under different circumstances from those in which we are living to-day, there went up a cry from the hidden depths of human nature for a re-formation of human social relations.   Through all the scheme of the new order ran like a motto the three words, Fraternity, Equality, Liberty.   Of course, no one with an unprejudiced mind and normal human feeling for the realities of human evolution can fail to sympathise with all that these three words imply.   But still, in the course of the nineteenth century there were keen thinkers who were at pains to point out the impossibility of realising the three ideas of brotherhood, equality and freedom in any homogeneous and uniform order of society.   It seemed to them clear, that these three impulses must contradict one another in social life, if carried actually into practice. It was, for instance, very cleverly demonstrated, that if the impulse towards e q u a l i t y were r e a l i s e d there would be no possible room for that freedom which is so inherent in every human being. And whilst one cannot but agree with those who see the contradiction between them, yet at the same time, one's human sympathies must go out to all and each of these three ideals in itself!

These three ideals appear contradictory, until one perceives the necessity for establishing a threefold order of society; and then their real meaning for social life first becomes apparent. The three divisions must not be artificially dovetailed together and centralised under some theoretical scheme of unity, parliamentary or other. They must be one living reality. Each of the three branches of the body social must centre in itself; and the unity of the whole will first come about through the workings of the three, side by side and in combination. For in actual life it is the apparent contradictories that make up a unity. Accordingly, one will come to comprehend what the life of the body social is, when one fully perceives the part played by these three principles of brotherhood, equality and freedom in a real, workable form of society. It will then be recognised, that men's co-operation in *economic* life must rest on that *brotherhood* that springs out of the Associations. The second system is that of *"common rights,"* where one is dealing with purely human relations between one person and another; and here one must strive to realise the idea of *equality*. Whilst in the *spiritual* field, which stands comparatively alone within the body social, it is the idea of *freedom* that needs to be realised. Seen in this way, these three ideals reveal their value for real existence. Thy cannot find their realisation in a chaotic stream of social life, but only in the threefold working of a healthy social organism. No social state, constructed on an abstract centralised scheme, can carry freedom, equality and brotherhood pall mall into practice. But

each of the three branches of the body social can derive its strength from one of
these ideal impulses; and then all three
branches will work fruitfully in conjunc-
tion.

Those people who, at the end of the
eighteenth century, first demanded the
recognition of these three ideas, Freedom,
Equality, Brotherhood, and those who
took up the cry again later on,—they had
already a dim sense of whither the forces
of human evolution were tending in modern times. But they had not got beyond belief in the onefold State. And in the onefold State these ideas involve a contradiction. They pinned their faith to the contradiction, because, deep-down in the sub-
conscious depths of their souls, there was
this striving towards the threefold order
of society, in which their trinity of ideas
can actually achieve a higher unity. To
lay hold on those evolutionary forces,
which through the growth of mankind all
through these latter times, are working
towards the threefold order,—to make of

them a conscious social will and purpose,—
this is what is demanded of us at the present day in unmistakeable language by the
hard facts of the social situation.

III.

Capitalism and Social Ideas
(Capital and Human Labour)

To form an opinion as to what the course of action is in the social field, which the facts of the day are so loudly demanding, is only possible, if one is willing to be guided in one's opinion by an insight which goes below the surface, to the fundamental forces of the social organism. The following introductory remarks are the outcome of an effort to arrive at such an insight. Nothing profitable can be done in the present day with social measures based on opinions that are drawn from a restricted sphere of observation. The facts that have grown out of the social movement reveal disturbances at the foundations of the social order, not merely surface ones. And to cope with these facts one needs an insight that also goes to the root of things.

Capital and Capitalism, as talked of to-day, indicates something in which the working-class portion of mankind look for the cause of their grievances. But to come to any profitable conclusion as to the part played by capital within the social processes, whether for good or ill, one must first be perfectly clear as to the way in which capital is produced and consumed, through the agency of men's individual abilities, of the "rights" system, and of the forces of economic life. *Human labour* one talks of, as the thing that, together with capital and the nature-basis of industry, goes to the creation of economic values, and through which the worker becomes conscious of his social position. To arrive however at any conclusion, as to the proper way of working human labour into the whole social organism without injuring the worker's sense of self-respect as a human being, one needs to keep clearly in sight the relation that human labour bears, on the one hand to individual ability and its development, and on the other to the common sense of right, the "rights-consciousness."

At the present moment people are very justly asking: What is the most immediate step to be taken in order to satisfy the claims that the social movement has brought to the front? But there is no taking even the most immediate step to good purpose, without first k n o w i n g how what one is trying to do is related to the fundamental principles of a healthy social order. And once one knows this, then, in whatever place one may find oneself, or whatever place one may select to work in, one will discover the particular task that requires doing under the circumstances. The obstacle to acquiring the kind of insight implied here, lies in that element of human will-power, which during the slow course of years has crystallised into social institutions. Men have so grown into these institutions, that the institutions themselves form the standpoint from which they view them and consider, what to change and what to leave. Their thoughts follow the lead of the facts, instead of mastering them.

To-day, it is necessary to see, that one cannot form any judgment adequate to the facts, without going back to those p r i m a l c r e a t i v e t h o u g h t s which underlie all social institutions. The body social requires a constant fresh supply of the forces that reside in these primal thoughts; and if the suitable channels are not there, through which these forces can flow, then social institutions assume forms which impede life, instead of furthering it. But although the conscious thoughts of men may go astray, although they may,—and have,—created facts that impede life, yet these primal thoughts live on in men's instinctive impulses. Tumultuously and destructively they break against the world of established facts that hem them in; and these primal thoughts it is, which open or

disguised, find their way out in convulsions
that threaten to overthrow the social order.
Such revolutionary convulsions will not
cease to occur, until the body social takes
a form, in which there may be always both
an inclination to notice when any institution is beginning to deviate from its first
intention in those primal thoughts, and at
the same time the possibility of counter-
acting every such deviation before it becomes strong enough to be a danger.   In
our times, the actual conditions, throughout a wide range of human life, have come
to deviate very widely from what the
primal thoughts require.   And these primal
thoughts, as they live on in the impulses
of the human soul, are a commentary,—
a commentary that voices itself loudly
enough in facts,—of what has been taking
shape in the body social during the last
few centuries.   What is wanted, is good
will and vigorous resolution to turn again
to these primal thoughts.   We must not be
blind to the mischief that is done, especially
at this moment, by dismissing these primal

thoughts from the field of actual life as "unpractical generalities." The facts of life itself, and the claims of the working-class masses, afford a practical commentary on what the modern age has made of the body social. The task of our age, in face of these facts, is not merely to criticise, but to set about remedying them; which means going to the primal thoughts for the direction in which we must now *consciously* guide them. For the time is gone by, when the old instinctive guidance could suffice for mankind; what it could accomplish up till now, is now no longer enough.

One of the main questions raised by the practical criticisms of the times is this:— How is a stop to be put to the oppression which working-class humanity suffers under private capitalism. The owner, or controller, of capital is in a position to press other men's bodily labour into the service of any work he takes on hand? In the social relation that arises in the co-operation of capital and human labour-power, there are three elements to be distinguished: the *enterprising activity,* which must rest on the basis of individual ability in some one person or group of persons;— the relation of the "enterpriser" to the worker, which must be a "relation in right";—and the production of an object which acquires a commodity value in the circuit of economic life. For the "enterprising" activity to find its scope in a healthy way in the social order, there must be forces at work in social life which afford men's individual abilities the best possible mode of manifesting themselves; and therefore there must be one province of the body social which secures a person of ability free occasion for the employment of his abilities, and makes it possible to leave the estimation of their value to other people's free and voluntary understanding.

It is obvious, that the social activities, which a man is enabled to exercise by means of capital, fall within that domain of the body social which takes its laws and administration from the spiritual life. If the political State interferes to influence

these personal activities, then it is un-
avoidable that its influence should involve
a disregard of individual abilities. For the
political State is necessarily based on what
is similar and equal in all men's claims in
life; and it is its business to translate this
equality into practice. Within its own domain, the State must ensure every man having a fair chance to make his personal
opinion tell. For the work the State has
to do, the question of understanding or not
understanding individualities does not
come in; and therefore whatever the State
does towards realising its own principles
ought not to have any influence upon the
exercise of men's individual abilities. Nor
should it be possible for the prospect of
economic advantage to determine the exercise of individual ability where capital is
needed. Many persons in weighing the
pros and cons of capitalism lay great stress
upon this economic advantage. In their
opinion, it is only through the incentive
which this gives to individual ability that
individual ability can be induced to exert

itself; and they refer, as "practical men" to the "imperfections of human nature," with which they claim to be well acquainted. No doubt, in that social order, under which the present state of things matured, the prospect of economic advantage has come to play a very important part, and is in no small measure the very cause of that state of things, of which we are now feeling the effects, and which calls for the development of some other, different incentive to the exercise of individual ability. This incentive must lie in the "social sense," that will spring from a healthy spiritual life. Strong in the freedom of the spiritual life, a man's education and schooling will send him forth equipped with impulses, that will lead him, thanks to this social sense, to realise the bent of his personal abilities.

There is not necessarily anything high-flown or visionary about such a belief. No doubt high-flown illusions have wrought immeasureable harm in social endeavour, as in other fields. But all that has been said before is enough to shew, that the view here urged is not based on any fanciful notion that "the spirit" will work wonders, provided the "spiritually-minded" only talk enough about it. It is the outcome of observation, of watching how people actually work, when they work together freely in the spirtiual field. This work in common, takes, of its own nature, a social character, *provided it can develope in real freedom.*

It is only the lack of freedom in spiritual life, which has kept its social character in abeyance. The fashion in which the forces of social life have found expression amongst the leading classes, has restricted their use and value to limited circles of mankind, in a way which is anti-social. What was produced in these circles could only be brought artificially within reach of working-class mankind. This section of mankind could draw no strength for the support of their souls from this spiritual life; for they had no real part nor property in it. Schemes for "popular instruction,"

for "the uplifting of the masses," "Art for
the People," and so forth,—all such things
are not really the means of spreading spiritual property amongst the people, whilst
spiritual property keeps the character it
has acquired in recent times. For "the
people," as regards their inmost life and
being, *are not in it*. All that it is possible
to give them, is as it were a bird's-eye
view of these spiritual treasures from a
point outside. And if this is true of spiritual life in its narrower sense, it has also
its meaning for those offshoots of spiritual
activity, which find their way into economic
life on the basis of capital. In a sound
order of society, the worker will not stand
at his machine, and come into contact with
nothing but its mechanism; whilst the capitalist alone knows what is the destiny of
the manufactured commodities in the
round of economic life. The workman
must share fully in the whole concern, and
be able to form a distinct conception of
the part that he himself is playing in social
life through his work in making the com-

modity. The enterpriser must hold regular conferences, with the object of arriving at a common field of ideas that shall include both employers and employed. Such conferences must be regarded as being as much a part of the business as the actual work. This is a healthy way of conducting business, and one that will arouse in the workers a sense, that by the control of capital, if he uses it properly, a person benefits the whole community,— including the worker, as a member of it. The above-board dealing, necessary to a willing understanding on the part of others, will make the "enterpriser" careful to keep his business methods above suspicion.

All this will not seem negligible to anyone with a sense for the social effects of that inner community of feeling and experience, which arises from the prosecution of a common task. Those who possess this sense, will clearly perceive, how greatly it is to the benefit of economic activity that the direction of economic affairs, based on capital, should come from the spiritual life, and have its roots in the spiritual domain. This preliminary condition must be fulfilled, before people's present interest in capital and in increasing it simply for the sake of profits, can give place to an interest in the actual business of production and the doing of the job on hand.

Persons of a socialist turn of mind at the present day aim at bringing the means of production under the control of the community. What is right and desirable in their aims can only be achieved if this control is exercised through the free spiritual domain. Such control through the free spiritual domain will do away with all possibility of that economic coercion, which brings with it such a sense of degradation, and which the capitalist exerts when his capitalist activities are born and bred of the forces of economic life; and it will also prevent that crippling of men's individual abilities, which inevitably results when these abilities are directed by the political State.

Earnings on everything done through capital and individual ability must depend in a healthy social order, like all other spiritual work, on the free initiative of the doer and on the free appreciation of those who wish the work done. The estimate of what these earnings should be, must, in this field, be in accordance with a man's own free view—on what he is willing to regard as a suitable return on his work, taking into consideration the preliminary training he requires for it, the incidental expenses to which he is put, etc., etc. Whether he finds his claims gratified or not, will depend on the appreciation his services meet with.

Social arrangements on the lines here proposed will lay the basis for a really free contractual relation between the work-director and the work-doer,—a relation resting not on barter of commodities (or money) for labour-power, but on an agreement as to the share due to each of the two joint authors of the commodity.

The sort of service, that is rendered to

the body social on the basis of capital, depends of its very essence on the part played in it by men's individual abilities. Nothing but the free spiritual life can give men's abilities the impulse they need for their development. Even in a society, where the development of individual ability is tied up with the administration of the political State, or to the forces of economic life, even there, real productivity, in everything requiring the expenditure of capital depends on as much of free individual power as can find its way through the shackles imposed upon it. Only, under such conditions, the development is an unhealthy one. It is not the free development of individual ability, exercised on a basis of capital, that has brought about conditions under which human labour-power can be nothing but a commodity; it is the shackling of these powers through the political life of the State or in the circuit of economic processes. An unprejudiced recognition of this fact is at the present day a necessary first step to everything that has to be done in the field of social organisation. For the superstition has grown up in modern times, that the measures needed for the welfare of society must come from either the political State or the economic system. And if we pursue any further the road along which this superstition has started us, we shall set up all manner of institutions, that, far from leading man to the goal towards which he is striving, will increasingly aggravate the oppressive conditions from which he is seeking to escape.

At the time when people first began to think about the question of capitalism, this same capitalism had already set up a disease in the body social. The disease is what people feel and are aware of. They see that it is something which has to be counteracted. But one must see further than that; one must recognise, that the origin of the disease lies in the fact, that the creative forces, at work in capital, have been absorbed into the circuit of economic life. If one is to work in the direction already urgently demanded by the evolutionary forces of mankind, one must not suffer oneself to be deluded by the type of thought, which regards as an unpractical piece of idealism the demand, that the spiritual life should be set free, and given control of the employment of capital.

At the present moment, certainly, people seem but little disposed to connect the spiritual life in any way directly with that social idea, which is to put capital on sound lines. They try to connect onto something that falls within the circuit of economic life. They see, that the manufacture of commodities in recent times has led to wholesale dealing, and this again to the present form of capitalism. And now they propose to replace this form of industrial economy by a syndical system, under which the producers will be working for their own wants. But since of course industry must retain all the modern means of production, the various industrial concerns are to be united together into one big syndicate. Here, they think, everyone will be producing to the orders of the community, and the community cannot be an exploiter, because it would simply be exploiting itself.   And for the sake, or from the necessity, of linking onto something that already exists, they turn their eyes on the modern State, with a view to converting this into a comprehensive syndicate.   One thing however they leave out of their reckoning, namely, that the bigger the syndicate the less possibility there is of its being able to do what they expect of it.   Unless individual ability finds its place in the syndical organism in the manner and form already described, it is impossible that communal control of labour should result in a healthy commonwealth.

The reason why people are so ill-disposed to-day to form an unbiassed opinion as to the position spiritual life occupies in the social order, is that they are accustomed to think of what is spiritual as being at the opposite end from all that is material and practical.   Not a few will find something rather absurd in the view here put forward, that the employment of capital in economic

life must be regarded as the way in which
one side of the spiritual life manifests itself. It is conceivable, that in characteris-
ing what is here said as absurd, members
of the late ruling classes may even find
themselves in agreement with socialist
thinkers. If one would see all that this
supposed absurdity means for the health
of the body social, one must examine certain currents of thought in the present day,
—currents of thought, which spring from
impulses in the soul, that are quite honest
after their fashion, but which nevertheless,
wherever they find entrance, check the development of any really social way of
thinking.

These currents of thought tend more or
less unconsciously away from all that gives
due energy and driving power to the inward life. They make for a conception
of life,—an inner life of thought, of soul,
directed to the pursuit of knowledge,—
which shall be as it were an island in the
common sea of human existence. Thus
they are not in a position to build the bridge

between this inner life and that other which binds men to the everyday world.   It is not uncommon to-day, to find persons who think it rather "distinguished" to sit aloft in castles of cloudland, meditating in somewhat pedantic abstractness over all manner of ethico-religious problems.   One finds them meditating on virtue and how a man may best acquire it; how he should dwell in loving-kindness towards his neighbours, and how he may be so blessed as to find "a meaning in life."   And, all the time, one recognises the impossibility of bridging the gulf between what these folks call good, and sweet, and kindly, and right, and proper, and all that is going on in the outer world amongst men's everyday surroundings, in the manipulation of capital, the payment of labour, the consumption, production and circulation of commodities, the system of credit banking, and the stock-exchange.   One can see two main streams running side by side even in men's very habits of thought, one of which remains up aloft as it were in divine spiritual altitudes, and has no desire to build a bridge from spiritual impulses to life's ordinary affairs. The other stream runs on, void of thought, in the everyday world. But life is a single whole. It cannot thrive unless the forces that dwell in all ethical and religious life bring driving power to the most commonplace, everyday things of life, into the sort of life that some persons may think rather beneath them. For, if people neglect to build the bridge between the two regions of life, then not only their religious and moral life, but their social thinking too, degenerates into mere wordy sentiment, far removed from commonplace, true realities. And then these commonplaces have their revenge as it were. For there is then still a sort of "spiritual" impulse in man, urging him in pursuit of every imaginable ideal and every conceivable thing that he calls "good"; whilst on the other side there are those different instincts, which are in opposition to these ideals,—the instincts that underlie the ordinary daily needs of life and require an economic system for their satisfaction, and to which he devotes himself *minus* his spirit. He knows no practicable path from his conception of spirituality to the business of everyday life. And so everyday life acquires a form, which is not even supposed to have any connection with those ethical impulses that remain aloof in the more distinguished altitudes, all soul and spirit. And then, the daily commonplaces are avenged; for the ethical religious life turns to a living lie in men's hearts, because, all unperceived it is being dissevered from commonplace practice and from all direct contact with life.

How many people there are to-day, who, from a certain ethical or religious distinction of mind, have all the will to live on a right footing with their fellow-men, who desire to act by others only in the best conceivable way, and yet fall short of the kind of feeling that would enable them to do so, because they cannot lay hold upon any social conception that finds its outlet in practical habits of life! It is people

such as these, who, at this epoch-making
moment in the world's history when social
questions have become so urgent, are block-
ing the road to a true practice of life. They
reckon themselves very practical persons,
and all the time are visionary obstruction-
ists. One can hear them making speeches
like this: "What is really needed, is for
people to rise above all this materialism,
this external material life which drove us
into the disaster of the great war and into
all this misery. They must turn to a spiritual conception of life." And to illustrate
man's path to spirituality, they are forever
harping upon great men of byegone days,
who were venerated for their conversion
to a spiritual way of thinking. One finds,
however, that directly one tries to bring the
talk round to the very thing that the spirit
has to do for real practical life, and what
is so urgently required of the spirit to-
day: the creation of daily bread, one is at
once reminded, that the first thing, after
all, is to bring people again to acknowledge
the spirit. At this moment however, the

urgent thing is, to employ the powers of
the spiritual life to discover the right principles of social health. And for this it is
not enough that men should make a hobby
of the spirit, as a bye-path in life. Everyday existence needs to be brought into line
with the spirit. It was this taste for turning spiritual life into bye-paths, that led
the late ruling classes to find their pleasure
in social conditions that ended in the present state of affairs.

In the social life of the present day, the
control of capital for the production of
commodities is very closely bound up with
the ownership of the means of production,
amongst which capital is of course in-
cluded. And yet these two relations between man and capital are quite different
as regards the way they operate within the
social system. The control of capital by
individual ability is, when suitably applied,
a means of enriching the body social with
wealth which it is to everyone's interest
should exist. Whatever a person's position in life, it is to his interest that nothing

should be wasted of those individual abilities which flow from the fountain-head of human nature, and through which things are created that are of use to the life of man.   These abilities, however, never become developed, unless the human beings endowed with them have free initiative in their exercise.   Any check to the free flow from these sources means a certain measure of loss to the welfare of mankind. Now capital is the means of making these abilities available for extended fields of social life.   It must be to the true interests of everybody in a community to have the collective property in capital so administered, that individuals specially gifted in one direction, or groups of people with special qualifications, should be able to acquire the use of capital, and should use it in the way their own particular initiative prompts them.   Everybody, be he brainworker or labourer, if he consults his own interests without prejudice, must say: "I should not only wish an adequate number of persons, or groups of persons, to have absolutely free use of capital, but I should also like them to have access to capital on their own initiative; for they themselves are the best judges of how their particular abilities can make capital a means of producing what is useful to the body social."

It does not fall within the scope of this work to describe how, in the course of mankind's evolution, as individual human abilities came to play a part in the social order, private property also grew up out of other forms of ownership. Ownership has, under the influence of the division of labour, gone on developing in this form within the body social down to the present day. And it is with present conditions that we are here concerned, and with what the next stage in their evolution must be. But in whatever way private property arose,—by the exercise of power, conquest, etc.,—it is an outcome of the social creativeness which is associated with individual human ability. And yet socialists to-day, with their thoughts bent upon social reconstruction, hold the theory, that the only way to ob-

viate what is oppressive in private ownership, is to turn it into communal ownership.   They put the question thus: How
can private property in the means of production be prevented from arising, so that
its oppressive effect upon the unpropertied
masses may cease?   In putting the question in this way, they overlook the fact,
that the social organism is something that
is constantly *changing, growing*.   One
cannot ask about a *growing* organism.
What is the best form of arrangement to
preserve it in the state which one regards
as the suitable one for it.   One can think
in that way about something which starts
at a certain point and then goes on in the
same way ever afterwards without any
essential change.   But that will not do for
the body social.   Its life is a continual
changing of each thing as it arises.   To
fix on some form as the very best, and expect it to remain in that form, is to under-
mine the very conditions of its life.

One of the conditions of life for the
body social is, that whoever can serve the

community through his individual abilities should not be deprived of the power to do so freely of his own initiative. Where such service involves free use of the means of production, to hamper free initiative would be to injure the general social interests. I am not proposing here to urge the argument commonly used in this connection, namely, that the prospect of the gains associated with the ownership of means of production is needed in order to stimulate the "enterpriser" to exertion. The whole form of thought represented in this book, with its conception of a progressive evolution in social conditions, must lead to the expectation, that this kind of incentive to social activity may be eliminated, through the emancipation of the spiritual life from its association with the political and economic system. Once it is free, the spiritual life will of itself inevitably evolve a social sense; and this social sense will provide incentives of a very different kind from the hope of economic advantage. But it is not so much a question of the

kind of impulse which makes men like private ownership of the means of production,
as of whether the necessary conditions of
life for the body social are best fulfilled
when the use of the means of production
is free, or when it is directed by the community. And here, one must always clearly
remember, that one cannot draw conclusions for the social organism of the present
day from the conditions of life supposed
to be found in primitive communities, but
from such only as correspond to man's
present stage of development. At the present stage, it is not possible for individual
ability to find fruitful exercise through
capital in the round of economic life, unless its use of capital is free. For fruitful results in any field of production there
must be opportunity for the free use of
capital; not because it gives an advantage
to some individual or group; but because,
opportunely directed by a social sense, it
is the best way of serving the community.
Whether he is producing alone or in company, the material a man is working on

is in a manner bound up with himself,
much like the skill of his own arms or legs.
To interfere with his free use of the means
of production, is like crippling the free
exercise of his bodily skill.   Private ownership, however, is simply the medium for
this free use of the means of production.
As regards ownership, all that matters to
the body social, is that the owner should
have the r i g h t to use it of his own free
initiative.   Clearly, two things are joined
together in social life, that are of quite
distinct implications for the body social—
one, the *free use* of the capital basis of
social production; the other, the *"relation
in right"* which arises between the user of
capital and other people, from the fact that
his right of use precludes these other people from free activity on this same capital
basis.

*It is not the free use of itself in the be-
ginning,* which does the mischief in society,
but *the continuance of the right of use*
after the circumstances have come to an
end which linked that use opportunely to

individual abilities.   Anyone who looks
upon the social organism as a changing,
growing thing, cannot fail to see what is
meant.   He will look about for some possible mode of arranging what is helpful
to life in one way, so that it may not have
bad effects in another.   For a live thing,
there is no possible mode of arrangement,
that can lead to fruition, in which the fin-
ished process in its growth will not in turn
become detrimental.   And if one is oneself to collaborate at a growing organism,
—as man necessarily must in the body social,—one's business cannot lie in checking
necessary developments, for the sake of
obviating detrimental consequences.   That
would be to sap every possibility of life
for the body social.   It is solely a question
of intervening at the right moment, when
what was helpful and opportune is beginning to turn detrimental.

Free use of the capital-basis through individual ability:—this must be an established possibility.   The ownership right involved in it must be shiftable, directly this

right begins to turn to a means of unrightfully acquiring power. There is one institution, introduced in our times, which partially meets this social requirement, though only for what one may call "spiritual property." "Spiritual property" when its author is dead, passes after a while into the ownership of the community for free use. Here we have an underlying conception, that is in accordance with the actual nature of life in a human society. Closely as the production of a purely spiritual possession is bound up with the private endowment of the individual, yet this possession is, at the same time, a result of the common social life, and must pass at the right moment into the common life. But it is just the same with other property. By aid of his property the individual person produces for the service of the community; but this is only possible in co-operation with the community. And accordingly the right to the use of a piece of property cannot be exercised apart from the interests of the community. The problem is not, how to abolish ownership of the capital-basis? but, how can ownership be best turned to the service of the community?

The way to do so, is to be found in the threefold order of society. The people combined in the threefold order act as a collective community through the "rights-State." The exercise of individual abilities comes under the spiritual organisation.

Everything in the body social indicates the necessity of introducing this threefold organic arrangement, when regarded with a sense of actualities, and not from a view entirely dominated by subjective opinions, theories, predilections, and so forth;—and this question of the relation of individual abilities to the capital-basis of economic life and its ownership, is a special case in point. The "rights-State" will not interfere with the formation and control of private property in capital, so long as the connection of the capital-basis with personal ability remains such, that this private control implies a service to the total community. Moreover, it will remain a "rights-State" in respect to its dealings with private property. It will never itself take over the ownership of private property. It will only ensure that the right of use is transferred at the right moment to a person or group of persons, who, again, through individual conditions, are capable of establishing a purely personal relation to this ownership. This will benefit the body social in two different aspects. The democratic foundation of the "rights-State," being concerned with the everything that touches *all men equally,* will enable a sharp watch to be kept, that property *rights* do not in course of time become property *wrongs.* And again,—(since the State does not itself administer property, but ensures its transference to individual ability),— men's individual abilities will develope their fructifying power for the whole body of the community. Under an organisation of this sort, property rights, or their exercise, can safely be left attached to a personality, for so long as seems opportune. One can conceive the representatives in the "rights-

State" laying down quite different regulations at different times as to the way in
which property is to be transferred from
one person or group to another.   At the
present day, when private property has
come to be regarded altogether with great
distrust, the proposal is, to convert private
property wholesale into communal property.   If people proceed far enough along
this road, they will find out, that they are
strangling the life of the community; and,
taught by experience, they will then pursue
a different path.   But it would undoubtedly
be better now, at once, to take measures
that would secure social health on the lines
here indicated.

So long as an individual alone, or in
combination with a group, continues to
carry on that productive activity which
first procured him a capital-basis to work
on, so long he shall retain the right to use
accumulations of capital arising as business
gains on the primary capital where the
gains are applied to the productive extension of the business.   Directly this par-

ticular personality ceases to control the
work of production, the accumulation of
capital shall pass on to another person, or
group, to carry on the same kind of business, or some other branch of productive
industry useful to the whole community.
Capital also, that accrues from a productive
industry but is not used for its extension,
must from the beginning go the same way.
Nothing shall count as the personal property of the individual directing the business, except what he receives in accordance
with the claim he made when he first took
over the business—claims, which he felt
able to make on the ground of his personal
abilities, and which appear justified by the
fact, that he was able to impress people
with his abilities sufficiently for them to
trust him with capital. If through his personal exertions the capital has been increased, then a portion of this increment
will pass into his private ownership,—the
addition so made to his original earnings
representing a percentage on the addition
to the capital. Where the original control-

ler of an industry is unable, or unwilling, to continue in charge, the capital used to start it will either pass over to the new controller with all incumbent obligations, or else will revert to the original owners, according as these latter may decide.

In such an arrangement, one is dealing with transfers of a right. The legal regulation of the terms on which such transfers shall take place, is a matter for the "rights-State." It will be for the "rights-State" also to see that these transfers are carried out and to conduct the process. It is conceivable that, in detail, the regulations laid down for any such transfer of a right will take very various forms, according as the common sense of right (the "rights-consciousness") varies in its view of what is right. No mode of conception, which, like the present one, aims at being true to life, will ever attempt to do more than indicate the general direction that such regulation should take. If one keeps to this direction and uses one's understanding, one will always, in any concrete instance discover what is the appropriate thing to do. One must judge always from the special circumstances and according to the spirit of the thing, what the right course is in actual practice. The more true to life any mode of thought is, the less it will attempt to lay down hard-and-fast rules for details, from preconceived notions of what is requisite. On the other hand, the very spirit of such a form of thought will lead necessarily and decisively to one result or another. For instance, it results unquestionably from such a mode of thought, that the "rights-State" must never use its control of rights-transfers to get any capital into its own hands. Its only business will be to see, that the transfer is made to a person, or group, whose individual abilities seem to warrant it. This at once presupposes also, as a general principle, that anyone, who is proposing to effect a transfer of capital under the circumstances described, will be at liberty to select his successor in the use of it. He will be free to select a person or group of

people, or else to transfer the right of use
to a corporate body belonging to the spiritual organisation.   For anyone, who has
rendered   practical   services   to   society
through his management of capital is a
person likely to judge from native ability
and with social sense, what should be done
with the capital afterwards.   And it will
be more advantageous to the community to
go upon what he decides, than to discard
his judgment, and leave the decision to
persons who have no direct connection with
the matter.

Some settlement of this kind will be required in the case of capital accumulations
over a certain amount, which have been
acquired by persons, or groups, through
the means of production (including land),
—except where these accumulations become private property by the terms originally agreed upon for the exercise of individual ability.

In this latter case, what is so earned, as
well as all savings that spring from the
results of a person's own work, will remain

until the owner's death, or some later date, in the private possession of the earner or his descendants. Until this date also, these savings will draw an interest from the person who is given them to procure the means of production. The amount of the interest will be the outcome of the general "rights-consciousness," and be fixed by the "rights-State." In a social order, based on the principles here described, it will be possible to effect a complete distinction between proceeds that are due to the employment of means of production, and sums accumulated through the earnings of personal labour, spiritual or physical. It is in accordance with the common sense of right, as well as to the general social interest, that these two things should be kept distinct. What a person saves and places at the disposal of a productive industry, is a service rendered to the general interests, inasmuch as it makes it possible in the first place for personal ability to direct production. But where, after deducting the rightful interest, there is an increase on the capital, arising out of the means of production, such increase is due to the collective working of the whole social organism, and must accordingly flow back into it again in the way above described. All that the "rights-State" will have to do, is to pass a resolution, that the capital accumulations in question are to be transferred in the prescribed way. It will not be called on to decide, which material or spiritual branch of production is to have the disposal either of capital so transferred or of capital savings;—for this would lead to the State tyrannising over spiritual and material production, which are best directed for the body social by men's individual abilities, as has been shewn. But it will be open to anyone to appoint a corporate body of the spiritual organisation to exercise the right of disposal over capital that he has created, if he does not want himself to select his successor.

Property acquired through saving, together with the interest on it, will also pass at the earner's death, or a while later, to some person or group actively engaged in spiritual or material production,—but only to a producer, not to be turned into an income by someone who is not producing. The choice will be made by the earner in his last will. Here again, if no person or group can be chosen direct, it will be a question of transferring the right of disposal to a corporation of the spiritual system. Only when a person himself makes no disposition of his savings, then the "rights-State" will act on his behalf, and require the spiritual organisation to dispose of them.

In a society ordered on these lines, due regard is paid both to private initiative on the part of the individual and at the same time to the social interests of the general community. Indeed the latter receive their full satisfaction through private initiative being set free to serve them. Whoever has to entrust his labour to the direction of another person, can at least know, under such an order of things, that their joint work will bear fruit to the best advantage of the community, and therefore of the worker himself.

The social order,—as here conceived,—will establish a proportionate relation, satisfactory to healthy human sense, between the prices of manufactured products and the two joint factors of their production,—namely human labour-power and these rights of use over capital (embodied in the means of production) which are subject to the common sense of right. No doubt all sorts of imperfections may be found in this. Imperfections do not matter. For a mode of thought that is true to life, what is of importance is not to lay down a perfect and complete programme for all time, but to point out the *direction* for practical work. The special instances, discussed here, are simply intended as illustrations to map out the direction more clearly. Any particular illustration may be improved upon; and this will be all to the good, provided the right direction is observed.

Through social institutions of this kind, personal and family feelings will admit of being brought into harmony with the claims of general humanity. It may of course be pointed out, that there will be a great temptation for people to transfer their property during their life-time to their descendants, or to some one of them, and that it is quite easy to give such a person the appearance of a producer, whilst all the while he may be quite incompetent compared to others, who would be much better in his place. The temptation to do this, can however be reduced to a minimum under social institutions of the above kind. The "rights-State" has only to require, that property, which is transferred from one member of a family to another, should under all circumstances, be made over to a corporation of the spiritual system, after the lapse of a certain period from the first owner's death. Or an evasion of the rule may be prevented in some other way by rights-law. The "rights-State" will merely see to it, that the property *is* so made over. The spiritual organisation must make provision for the choice of the person to in-

herit it. In the fulfillment of these principles a general sense will grow up, that the
next generation must be trained and educated to fit them for the body social and
that one must not do social mischief by
passing capital on to persons who are non-
productive. No one, in whom a real social sense is awakened, cares to have his
own connection with the capital basis of
his work carried on by any individual or
group whose personal abilities do not warrant it.

These proposals cannot be regarded as
a mere utopia by anybody who has a sense
of what is really practicable. For the kind
of institutions here proposed are such as
spring directly out of existing circumstances anywhere in life. Only, people will
have to make up their minds, gradually to
give up administering spiritual life and industrial economy within the "rights-State,"
and not to raise opposition, when private
schools and colleges are started and economic life put on its own footing,—seeing
that this is just what is wanted. There is

no need to abolish the State schools and the State economic undertakings straight away. But, beginning perhaps in quite a small way, it will be found increasingly possible to do away with the whole structure of State education and State economy.

This requires, however, first of all, individuals, convinced that these, or some such social ideas as these are the right ones, and able so thoroughly to imbue themselves with their rightness, that they will make it their business to spread them. Wherever such ideas find understanding, they will arouse confidence in the possibility of changing the present state of things into a healthy one, where the same evils will not arise. But this is the only kind of confidence which can lead to a really healthy state of things. For, before one can arrive at any such confidence, one must have a clear perception in what way, practically, it is possible to connect new institutions on to the existing old ones. The essential feature of the ideas here put forward would seem to be, that they do not propose to bring about a better future by destroying the present social order further than has already been done; but that their realisation will come through building upon what already exists; and that as the building-up process goes on, what is rotten and unsound will fall away. No new views nor teachings, that do not aim at establishing confidence in this respect, will attain the object which it is absolutely necessary to attain, namely, an unbroken course of evolution, in which all that men have hitherto achieved, the wealth they have worked for, and the faculties they have won, are not cast to the winds, but stored up. Even the most sweeping radical may feel confidence in a form of social reconstruction that still preserves the old heritage, when he has ideas laid before him which are capable of initiating really sane and healthy developments. Even he will have to recognise, that whatever class of men may get into power, they will not be able to remove existing evils, unless their impulses are supported by ideas that can put health and life into the body social. To despair,—to believe it impossible to find a sufficient number of people who, even in these days of turmoil will have understanding for these ideas, if only they are spread with enough energy,—this would be to despair of human nature and of its openness to healthful and purposeful impulses. Is it desperate? That is not the question to be asked. But rather, What must I do to give full force to the teaching and spread of ideas that can awaken men's confidence?

Any effective spread of these ideas will find its first obstacle in the habits of thought of the present age, which will quarrel with them on two grounds:—Either it will be objected in some form or another, that any dismemberment in the unity of the social life is inconceivable, that its three supposed branches cannot be torn apart, seeing that in actual practice they are everywhere intertwined. Or else people will opine, that it is quite possible under the onefold state to give each of the three branches its necessary independent

character; that all these ideas are mere
cobweb-spinning, with nothing in them,
and quite apart from all reality. The first
objection comes from thinking *unreally,*
from presupposing that unity of life is only
possible in a community of human beings,
when the unity is introduced by ordinance.
What life in reality requires is, however
just the reverse. Unity must be the *result,* the final outcome of all the streams of
activity flowing together from various directions. This idea is the one in accordance with life; but it had the evolution of
the latter age against it; and so the tide
of life in men bore down against the artificial "order" in its path,—and landed in
the present social conditions. The second
preconception arises from inability to distinguish the radical difference in the working of the three systems of social life. People do not see, that man stands in a separate and peculiar relation to each of the
three; that, for the full development of its
special quality, each of these three relations requires a ground to itself in actual

life, where it can evolve its own form apart from the other two, in order that all three may combine in their working.

There was a view held in time past by the physiocrats, that,—Either men make artificial government regulations for economic life, which check its free expansion,—and then these regulations are harmful;—Or else, the laws tend in the same direction as economic life does when left to itself,—and then they are superfluous. As an academic theory, this view has had its day; but it still crops up everywhere as a habit of thought, and plays havoc in men's brains. People think, that if one department of life is guided by its own laws, then everything else whatever that is needed in life must follow as a consequence out of this one department. That if, for instance, economic life were regulated in a way to satisfy men's wants, that then this well-ordered economic soil would infallibly produce the right sort of spiritual life and "rights" life as well. But it is not possible; and only a way of thinking

foreign to all reality can believe it possible.
In the circuit of economic life there is
nothing whatever that affords of itself any
motive to guide that which runs all through
the relation of man to man and proceeds
from the sense of right.   And if people
insist on regulating *this* relation by economic motive the result will be, that the
human being, with his labour and his control of the means of labour, will be bound
hand and foot to the economic life.   Economic life will go on like clockwork, and
man will be a wheel in it,"—Economic life
has a tendency always to go on in one course,
which needs rectifying from another side.
It is neither, that the "rights" regulations
are good, provided they move in the course
set by economic life—nor, that when they
run counter to it, they are bad.   But rather,
that if the course taken by economic life
is constantly under the influence of those
rules of "right" which concern man simply as man, then a human existence within
the economic life becomes possible.   And
not till individual ability grows on its own

ground, quite detached from the economic system, conveying ever afresh to economic life those forces that economics and industry are powerless to produce, can economic life itself develope in a way beneficial to men.   It is a curious thing:—in purely external matters, people are ready enough to see the advantage of a division of labour. They do not expect a tailor to milk his own cow.   But when it comes to a general division and co-ordination of human life, then they think that no good can come of anything but a onefold system.

———

That social ideas which follow the line of real life will rouse objections on every side, is a matter of course.   For real life breeds contradictions.   And anyone, who is thinking in accordance with life, will determine on realising arrangements that involve living contradictions, needing again other arrangements to reconcile them. *He must not suppose,* that an institution which is demonstrably, to his thinking, an "ideally perfect" one, will involve no contradictions when realised in practice. The socialism of the present day is absolutely justified in laying down the proposition, that the institutions of the modern age, in which production is carried on for individual profit, must be replaced by a different system, under which production shall be carried on for the general consumption. But anyone, who *fully and wholly* accepts this proposition will *not* arrive at the deduction drawn by modern socialism: *Ergo,* the means of production must be transferred from private to communal ownership. Indeed, he will be forced to a very different conclusion, namely, that right methods must be taken for conveying to the general community that which is privately produced on the strength of individual energy and capacity. The tendency of the economic impulses of the new age has been to obtain revenue by manufacturing in mass. The aim of the future must be, to find out, by means of Associations,

what, in view of the actual needs of consumption, is the best method of production,
and what channels are open from producer
to consumer.   The "rights" institutions
will take care, that a productive industry
does not remain tied up with any individual
or group of people longer than their personal ability warrants.   Instead of *communal ownership* of the means of production, there will be a *circulation* of the means
of production throughout the body social,
bringing them constantly afresh into the
hands of those persons whose individual
ability can employ them to the best service
of the community.   That connection between personality and the means of production, which hitherto has been effected
by private ownership, will thus be established for periods of time.   For it will be
thanks to the means of production that the
head of a business and his subordinates are
enabled by their personal abilities to earn
the income that they asked.   They will not
fail to make production as perfect as possible,   since   every   improvement   brings

them, not indeed the whole profits, but a portion of the returns. For profits,—as shewn above,—go to the community only to the extent of what is over, after deducting the quota due to the producer for improvements in production. And it is in the spirit of the whole thing, that, if production falls off, the producer's income must diminish in proportion as it rises with the enhancement of production. But always, in every case, the manager's income will come out of the spiritual work he has done. It will not come out of profits, depending on conditions that do not rest with the spiritual work of the directing personality, but with the interplay of the forces at work in the communal life.

It will be seen, that with the realisation of social ideas such as these, institutions that we already have will acquire an altogether new significance. The ownership of property ceases to be what it has been up till now. But instead of going back to an obsolete form, such as communal ownership would be, it is carried on a step further to something quite new. The objects of ownership are brought into the stream of social life. No private owner, for his own personal interests, can control them to the injury of the general public;—neither, again, can the general public control them bureaucratically to the injury of the private person;—but private persons, who are suitable, will have access to them, as a means of serving the public.

A sense for the general public interest will have a chance to grow up, when impulses of this sort are realised, which place production on a sound basis, and safeguards the body social from sudden crises. An administrature too, which occupies itself solely with the processes of economic life, will be able to bring about any adjustments for which necessity may arise in the course of these processes. Suppose, for instance, a business concern were not in a position to pay its creditors the interest due on the savings of their labour, then,—if it is a business that is nevertheless recognised as meeting a want,—it will be possible to arrange for other industrial concerns to subsidise it by the voluntary agreement of everyone concerned in them.

Self-contained, on a basis of "rights" determined from outside itself, and supplied from without by a constant flow of fresh human ability as it comes on the scenes, the economic life, within its own circuit, will concern itself with nothing but its proper work. Accordingly it will be possible for it to facilitate a distribution of wealth that will ensure each person receiving that which he is rightfully entitled to receive, according to the community's general prosperity. And, if one person appears to have more income than another, it will only be because his individual abilities make this More, this "surplus," of advantage to the community.

The taxes which are needed for the "rights" system can be settled between the leaders of the "rights" life and the eco-

nomic life in a social organism shaped by
the light of such conceptions as these.
Whilst everything needed for the maintenance of the spiritual organisation will
come as good-will from the voluntary appreciation of the private members of the
body social. The spiritual organisation
will rest on a healthy basis of individual
initiative, exercised in free competition
amongst the private individuals suited to
spiritual work.

But it is only in a social organism of
this form, that the "rights" administration will find the understanding necessary
to a right and just distribution of wealth.
In an economic life, where the claim upon
men's labour is not prescribed by the
stresses in single branches of production,
but which has to carry on business with
as much as the "rights-law" allows it, the
value of goods will be determined by what
men actually put into it in the way of work.
It will not allow the work men do to be
determined by goods-values into whose
formation human welfare and human dig-

nity do not enter. An order of economy
such as this, will not be blind to rights
that arise from purely human relations.
Children will have a right to education.
The father of a family will be able to have
a higher income than a single man. He
will get his "surplus" through a system
instituted by agreement between all three
social organisations. The right to education might be met, under these arrangements, in the following way. The man-
aging body of the economic organisation
estimates the amount of revenue that can be
given to education, according to the general economic conditions; and the "rights-
state" fixes the rights of individual persons,
according to the spiritual organisation's
opinion in each case.

Here again, since we are thinking on
lines of reality, this instance is merely intended to indicate the direction in which
such arrangements might be worked. In
detail, it is possible that quite a different
sort of arrangement may be found to be
the right thing. But, in any case, the

"right thing" will be found only through all three independent branches of the body social conjointly, in working together for a common end. For the purposes of this sketch, the underlying mode of thought is merely concerned to discover the really practical thing, (unlike so much to-day that passes for practical),—namely, a functional division of the body social, such as shall give man a basis on which to work socially to some purpose.

On a par with a child's right to education, is the right of the aged, of invalids, widows and sick persons, to a maintenance; and the capital-basis for their support will be passed through the three systems of the body social in much the same way as the capital contributed for the education of those who are not yet come to their working powers. The essential point in all this is, that the income received by anyone who is not personally an earner, should not be an outcome of the economic life; but the other way about:—economic life must be dependent on what is the outcome of the common sense of right. The people working in any economic organism will have all the less from their work, the more has to go to the non-earners; only the "less" will be borne fairly by all the members of the body social, when social impulses, of the kind here meant, are really put into practice. The education and maintenance of those who cannot work concerns all mankind in common; and under a "rights-state" detached from economic life it will become the common concern in actual practice. For the "rights" organisation is the field for realising those things *in which every grown human being has a voice.*

Under a social order, that follows this line of conception, the *surplus* that a man performs on the strength of his individual ability will pass on to the community; and the just maintenance for the *deficiency* of the less able will also come from the community. "Surplus value" will not be created for the unjustified enjoyment of private individuals, but to enhance everything that can give wealth of soul and body to the whole social organism, and to foster whatever is born of it, even though not directly serviceable.

It may be thought, that, after all, except for the idea of it, there is no practical value in keeping the three members of the body social thus carefully distinct, and that the same result would come about "of itself" inside a uniform constitution of State, or an economic guild covering the same ground as the state, and based on communal ownership of the means of production. One needs, however, only to look at the special form of social institution that must result from realising the threefold division. For instance, the use of money as a mode of payment will not have to be legally recognised by the state administrature. It will owe its recognition to the measures taken by the various administrative bodies within the economic organisation. For money, in a healthy social organism, can be nothing except an order on commodities that other people have produced, and which one can draw out of the common economic pool, because of the commodities that oneself has produced and paid in.   It is the money currency that makes a sphere of economic activity into an economic unit.   The whole economic life is a roundabout way of everyone producing for everyone else.   Within the sphere of economic activity, commodity-values are the only things dealt with; and in this sphere, not only anything *made,* but also anything *done,* originating in the spiritual or State organisations, also takes on the character of a commodity.   What a teacher does for his pupils, is, for the economic circuit, a commodity.   The teacher's individual ability is no more paid for, than the worker's labour-power is paid for.   All that can possibly be paid for in either, is that which proceeds from them and can pass as a commodity or commodities into the economic circuit.   How free initiative, and what the "rights-law" must act, in order to bring the commodity into existence, lies as much outside the economic circuit itself as the action of the forces of nature upon the corn yield in a bountiful or barren year. For the economic circuit, both the spiritual organisation,—as regards its claim on economic returns,—*and the State also,* are simply producers of commodities. Only, what they produce is not a commodity within their own spheres; it first becomes a commodity, when it is taken up into the economic circuit. Within their own domains, the spiritual organisation and the state have no business dealings;— the economic body, through its administrature, carries on business with their work when it is done.

The purely economic value of any commodity (or work done, in so far as it finds expression in the money that represents its equivalent value), will depend on the efficiency in *economic administration* developed by the body economic. It will depend on the measures taken by the economic administration, how fertile economic life can become on the basis afforded by the spiritual and "rights" systems of the body social. The money-value of a commodity will then indicate, that the economic organisation is producing the commodity in a quantity corresponding to the want for it.   Supposing the premises laid down in this book to be realised, the body economic will not be dominated by the impulse to amass wealth through sheer quantity of production; but the production of goods will adapt itself to wants, through the agency of the associative guilds that will spring up in all manner of connections.   In this way, the proportion, that in each case corresponds to the actual want, will become established between the money-value of an article and the arrangements made in the body social for producing it.(§§)   In the healthy so-

---

(§§).   *Author's Note.*   A sound proportion between the prices of made goods can only be achieved in economic life as an outcome of social administration, that springs up in this way from the free co-operation of the three branches of the body social.   The proportion between prices must be such, that anyone working receives as counter-value for what he has produced so much as is necessary to satisfy his total wants and the wants of those belonging to him, until he has again turned out a product of equivalent labour   It is impossible to fix such a price-relation officially in advance; *it must come as the resultant* of living co-operation be-

cial organism, money will really be nothing but a measure of value; since, behind every money piece, or money token, there stands the tangible piece of production, on the strength of which alone the owner of the money could come by it. These conditions will, of their nature, necessitate arrangements being made, which will deprive money of its value for its possessor, when once it has lost its original significance. Arrangements of this sort have already been alluded to. Money property passes back, after a fixed period, into the common pool, in whatever the proper form may be; and to prevent money, withdrawn from

---

tween the associations actively at work in the body social. Prices will however certainly settle down into such a normal relationship, provided the joint work of the associations rests on a healthy co-operation between the three divisions of social life. One may rely on the result as securely as on having a safe bridge, when it is built according to the proper laws of mathematics and mechanics. It may be said, that social life does not invariably obey its own laws, like a bridge. This facile objection however will not be made by anyone able to recognise, that it is primarily the *laws of life,* and not the laws of mathematics, which all through this book are conceived as underlying social life.

use in industry, being held back by its pos-
sessors to the evasion of the provisions
made by the economic organisation, there
can be a new coinage, or re-stamping, from
time to time.   One result of this will no
doubt be, that the interest derived from
any capital sum will diminish as years go
on.   Money will wear out, just as commodities wear out.   Nevertheless, such a
measure will be a right and just one for
the State to enact.   There can be no compound interest.   If a person lays by savings, he has certainly rendered past services that gave him a claim on future coun-
ter-service in commodities,—just as present services claim present service in exchange.   But his claims cannot go beyond
a certain limit; for claims, that date from
the past, require present labour-services to
satisfy them; and they must not be turned
into a means of economic coercion.   The
practical realisation of these principles will
put the problem of safeguarding the
money standard upon a sound basis. For,
no matter what form money may take ow-

ing to other conditions, the safeguard of
its standard lies in the intelligent organisation of the whole body economic through
its administrature. The problem of safeguarding the money standard will never
be satisfactorily solved through any State
by means of law. The present States will
only solve it, when they give up attempting
the solution on their own account, and leave
the body economic to do what is needful,
after it is detached from the State.

There is much talk of the modern division of labour, of its results in time-saving,
in perfecting the manufacture and facili-
tating the exchange of commodities. Little attention is paid to its effect on the relation of the human worker to what he is
doing. In a social order that is based on
division of labour, no person at work is
ever really earning his income himself, he
is earning it through the work of everybody employed in the body social. When
a tailor makes a coat for his own use, the
relation of himself to the coat he is making
is not the same as that of a man living

under primitive conditions, who has all the other necessaries of life to provide for himself. The tailor makes the coat in order to enable him to make clothes for other people; and its v a l u e for him depends solely and entirely on what services other people render. The coat is, really, a means of production. Many people may call this "splitting hairs";—but one sees that it is not so, when one comes to consider the formation of commodity-values in the economic process. It then becomes obvious, that in an economic organism based on division of labour it is absolutely impossible to work for oneself. All one can do, is to work for others, and set others to work for one. One can no more work for oneself, than one can eat oneself. One can, however, establish practices, that are in direct opposition to the very essence of division of labour;—as, for instance, when the whole system of goods-production is based on transferring to the individual as private property what he is only able to produce through occupying a place in the

social organism. Division of labour makes
for a social organism in which the individual shall live in accordance with the conditions of the whole body of the community. *Economically,* division of labour precludes egoism. And if, in spite of this,
egoism persists, in the form of class privi-
lege and such things, then a State of in-
stability sets in, leading to disturbances in
the body social. We are living under such
conditions to-day. To insist that the conditions in the "rights-State," amongst other
things, must bring themselves into line with
the system of divided labour and its non-
egotistic method of production, may appear
to many people futile. In this case, they
may as well draw the deduction from their
premises: There is no doing anything.
The social movement can lead to nothing.
As respects the social movement, one can
certainly do no good, unless one is willing
to give Reality her due. It is inherent in
the mode of thought underlying the whole
treatment of the subject, throughout these
pages, that man's doings within the body

social must be brought into line with the conditions of its organic life.

Anyone, who can only form his notions by the system he is accustomed to, will be uneasy when he is told, that the relation between the work-director and the worker is to be separated out from the economic process. He will believe that such a separation is bound to lead to depreciation of money and a return to primitive conditions of industrial economy.—(Dr. Rathenau takes this view in his "After the Flood"; and from his standpoint it is a defensible one.)—The threefolding of the social order, however, prevents any risk of this. The autonomous economic system, working conjointly with the "rights" system, completely detaches the whole state of money conditions from labour conditions, which latter rest entirely on the rights-law. The "rights" conditions cannot have any direct influence on the money conditions, for these are the result of the economic administration. The "relation in right" between work-director and worker will not upset the balance·or shew itself in money-values at all. For, when wages are eliminated, (which represent a relation of exchange between commodities and labour-power), money-value remains simply a measure of the value of one commodity (or piece of work) as against another. If one studies the threefold division in its actual effects upon the body social, one must become convinced that such a division will lead to institutions unknown to the forms of State that have existed up till now.

These new institutions can be cleared of all that to-day has an atmosphere of *class-struggle*. For this struggle comes from the wages of labour being tied up with the economic processes. Here, we are describing a form of social organism, in which the conception of *wages of labour* undergoes a transformation no less complete than the old conception of *property*. But the social relation of human-beings becomes

thereby a much more living and healthy
one.   One must not jump to the conclusion,
that these proposals amount in practice
merely to converting time-wages into piece-
wages.   One might be led to this conclusion by a one-sided view of the matter.
But this one-sided view is not that which
is put forward as the right one here.   Here,
we are considering, *in its connection with
the whole organisation of the body social,*
the elimination of the wage-relation altogether, and the adoption of a share-rela-
tion, based on contract in respect to the
common work performed by the work-
director and the workers.   It may seem
to somebody, that the portion of the proceeds which falls to the worker's share is
a "piece-wage"; but if so, it is because he
fails to see, that this kind of "piece-wage"
(which, properly speaking, is not a "wage"
at all) finds expression in the value of the
product in a way, that puts the worker socially into a position as regards the other
members of the body social very different
from that relation between him and them,

which has sprung out of class supremacy in which economics are the only factor. Class struggle finds no place here; and this requirement is satisfied.

And for those who hold the theory,—not infrequently to be heard in socialist circles, —that the course of "evolution" itself must bring the solution of the social question, that it is impossible to set up views and say that they ought to be realised,—to these we shall reply: Most certainly evolution will bring about that which must be; but men's ideas are r e a l i t i e s and active impulses within the body social. And when time has gone on a little further, and that has become *realised* which to-day can only be thought, then these realised thoughts will be there in the evolution. With time, when the thoughts of to-day have become part of evolution, then those, who look to "evolution alone" and have no use for fruitful ideas, may be better able to form a judgment. Only, when that time comes, it will be *too late* to accomplish certain things, which are required *now* by the facts of *to-day*.   In the social organism, it is not possible to set about observing the evolution from outside, objectively, as one does in nature.   One is obliged to take an active part in the evolutionary process.   And it is therefore so disastrous for all sound thought on social matters that it is to-day up against views that are bent on "demonstrating" social requirements as one "demonstrates" a fact in natural science.   In the comprehension of social life, there can be no "proof," unless one takes into account not only what is actually present existing, but also that other factor, latent within men's impulses, often unknown to themselves, seed-like and striving towards realisation.

One of the ways, in which the threefold system will shew that it is based on the essentials of human social life, will be the removal of the judicial function from the sphere of the State.   It will be for the

State institutions to lay down the rights that are to be observed between men or groups of men; but the passing of judgment comes within institutions proceeding from the spiritual organisation. In passing judgment, a very great deal depends on what opportunity the judge has for perceiving and understanding the particular circumstances of the person whom he is trying. Nothing can ensure this perception and understanding, except those ties of trust and confidence that draw men together in the institutions of the spiritual order, and which must be made the main consideration in appointing the courts of law. Possibly, the administrature of the spiritual organisation might nominate a panel of magistrates who could be drawn from the widest range of spiritual professions and would return to their own calling at the expiration of a certain period. Everybody then would have the opportunity, within certain limits, of selecting a particular person on the panel for five or ten years at a time,—someone in whom the

rhythmic system, which, to arrive at any
he feels sufficient confidence to be willing
to accept his verdict in a private or criminal
suit, if it came to the point. There would
always be enough magistrates, in the neigh-
borhood where anyone was residing, to
give a value to the power of selection. A
complainant would always have to apply
to the magistrate competent to the de-
fendant.

Only consider, what such an institution
would have meant for the territories of
Austria-Hungary! In districts of mixed
language, the member of any nationality
would have been able to choose a judge of
his own race. And anyone acquainted
with Austrian affairs will know, how
greatly such an arrangement might have
contributed to keep the balance in the life
of her various nationalities. But apart
from nationality, there are many fields of
life where such an arrangement might
have a beneficial effect on healthy development. For more detailed acquaintance
with points of law, the judges thus ap-

pointed and the courts will be assisted by
regular officials, whose selection will also
be determined by the spiritual administrature, but who will not themselves decide
cases.   The same administrature will also
have to constitute courts of appeal.   The
kind of life, that will go on under the conditions here supposed, will of its nature
bring a judge into touch with the mode of
life and feeling of those whom he has to
judge; his own life, outside the brief period
of judicial office, will make him familiar
with their lives and circles.   Everywhere
and in all its institutions, the healthy social
organism will draw out the social sense of
those who share its life,—and so too with
the judicature.   The execution of a sen-
tence is the affair of the "rights-State."

—————

It is not necessary for the moment here
to go into arrangements, entailed in other
fields of life as well by the realisation of
what has been put forward in these pages.

A description of them would obviously take up unlimited space.

The particular instances already given of the forms social life will take, should dispose of a notion, (which I have actually met with when lecturing on this subject in various places), that this is an attempt to revive the three old "estates" of the Plough, the Sword and the Book. What is here intended, is just the very opposite to this division into grades. Men will not be divided into functions of the body social, neither as Classes, nor Estates. It is the body social itself which will be functionally divided. And thereby man for the first time will be able to be truly man; for the three social divisions will be such, that he himself has his own life's roots in each of them. His calling gives him a footing in one of the three, and to this he belongs through his practical interests. And his relation to the other two will be a very actual and living one; for his connection with their institutions is of a kind to create such a living relation. Threefold

will be the body social, as apart from man
and forming the groundwork of his life;
and each man will unite its three divisions
within himself.

IV

International Aspects of the Threefold Commonwealth

The internal structure of a healthy social organism makes its international relations also threefold. Each of its three branches will have its own independent relation to the corresponding branch of other threefold organisms. All manner of interconnections will spring up between the economic network of one district and that of another, without being directly influenced by the connections between their "rights-States." (§§)   And, conversely, the rela-

---

(§§). *Author's Note.* It may be urged, that the "rights" relations and the economic relations form one indivisible whole in actual reality. This however misses the point of what is meant by the threefold division. Of course, in the mutual intercourse and exchange that

tions between their "rights-States" will, within certain limits, develope in complete independence of their economic connections.(§§) This independence of origin will enable these two sets of relations to act as a check upon each other in cases of dispute. Such a close interweaving of interests will grow up, as will make territorial frontiers seem negligible in the life of mankind.

The spiritual organisations of the different districts will become linked in a way that only the common spiritual life of mankind can make possible. Detached from the State and placed on its own footing, the spiritual life will develope all manner of connections, that are impossible when the recognition of spiritual services does not

---

goes on between the various social organisms, *taken as a collective process*, the two different sorts of relations,—between their "rights" systems and their economic systems,—work together as a single whole. But it is a different matter, whether one makes rights regulations to suit the requirements of economic intercourse, or whether one first shapes them by the common sense of right, and then takes the combined result, whatever it may be.

rest with a spiritual corporation, but with the "rights-State." So far as this is concerned, there is no real difference between the services rendered by science,—which are frankly international,—and those rendered in any other spiritual field. The common language of a nation, and all that goes along with language, constitutes one such field of spiritual life,—including the national consciousness itself. The people of one language-area do not come into unnatural conflict with those of another language-area, except when they try to make their national form of civilisation predominant through the use of their State-organisation or their economic power. If one national civilisation spreads more readily, and has greater spiritual fertility than another, then it is quite right that it should spread; and the process of spreading will be a peaceful one, provided it comes about solely through the agency of the spiritual communities of the different social organisms.

At the present time, the keenest opposition to the threefold order will come precisely from those groups of mankind which have clustered round a common origin of speech and national culture. Such opposition however must break down before the common goal of all mankind,—a goal towards which men will set their faces with increasing consciousness from the very necessities of life in the modern age. Mankind will come to feel, that each of its many parts can only lead a life worthy of their common humanity, when bound in living links to all the rest. National affinities, together with other impulses of a natural order, are amongst the causes which historically led to the formation of communities in "rights" and communities of industrial economy. But the forces to which nationalities owe their growth require for their development free mutual interaction, untrammelled by any ties that grow up between the respective bodies of State and the economic Associations. And the way of achieving this, is for the various national communities to develope the threefold order within their own social structures; and then their three branches can each expand its own relation with the corresponding branches of the other communities.

In this way, peoples, States, economic bodies, become grouped together *in formations that are very various in shape and character,* and every part of mankind becomes so linked with the other parts, that each is conscious of the life of the other pulsing through its own daily interests. *A league of nations is the outcome,*—arising out of root impulses that correspond to actual realities. There will be no need to "institute" one, built up solely on legal theories of right.(§§)

To anyone, who is thinking of these things in terms of real life, it must seem

---

(§§). *Author's Note.* Some people think these things "Utopias," because they fail to see that, in reality, actual life itself is struggling towards the very kind of arrangement which seems to them so Utopian, and that the actual mischief going on in real life is due precisely to the fact that these arrangements are nowhere to be found.

of especial importance, that the aims here set before the body social, whilst having a meaning for the whole of mankind collectively, are such as can be put in practice by any single corporate community, no matter what may be the attitude adopted by other countries for the time being.— If one corporate community has organised itself into its three natural divisions, the administratures of the three divisions can act together as a single body, and thus perfectly well form relations even with outside communities that are not yet prepared to adopt the threefold order themselves. Whoever leads the way with the threefold order, will be furthering the common aim of all mankind. What actually has to be done, will be carried through by that strength which an aim brings with it in practical life, when it is rooted in the actual guiding forces of humanity,—rather than by diplomatic agreements, or drafting schemes at conferences. It is on a basis of reality that this aim is conceived in thought. It is one to be pursued in the real action of life at any and every point amongst the communities of men.

Anyone, watching what was going on in the life of peoples and of States during the last 30 or 40 years from a point of view such as given in these pages, could see how the State-structures that had been built up in the course of history, with their blending of spiritual life, "rights" and industrial economy, were becoming involved in international relations that were heading for catastrophe. At the same time, it was equally plain, that the opposite forces at work within mankind's unconscious impulses were tending towards the threefold order. Here lies the remedy for those convulsions that have been brought about by the mania for unification. The way of life among the "leaders of mankind" was not however of the kind to enable them to see what had been for years past slowly working up. In the spring and summer of 1914, one still found "statesmen" saying, that, thanks to the governments' exertions, the peace of Europe was, so far as

could be humanly foreseen, assured. These
"statesmen" simply had not the faintest
notion, that all that they were doing and
saying had absolutely lost touch with the
course of real events. Yet these were the
people who were looked up to as "practical"; and people were regarded as little
better than "cranks" at that time, who had
been forming other views during all those
years, which differed from those of the
"statesmen";—such views, for instance, as
those expressed by the present writer
months before the war-catastrophe, when
addressing a small audience in Vienna,—
(a large audience would certainly have
laughed him down.) He then spoke of
the danger menacing, in more or less these
words:—"The tendencies prevalent in the
life of the present day will continue to
gather strength, until they end by annihi-
lating themselves. And if one reads social
life with the eyes of the spirit, one can perceive everywhere the ghastly signs of social tumours forming. Here is the great
menace to our civilisation, manifest to any-

one able to read below the surface of existence. It is this that is so appalling, so
overpowering, that—even if one could
otherwise repress all zeal on behalf of a
science in which spiritual knowledge is
made instrumental to the knowledge of
life's events,—these things alone would im-
pell one to speak, to proclaim the remedy,
to hurl one's words as it were in the face
of the world. If the body social follows
the same line of evolution as hitherto, it
will become full of sores—sores of civilisation that will be for it what cancers are for
man's natural body."—Such were the foundations upon which life rested, and which
the ruling circles neither could nor would
see. But their special view of life led them
to find in such conditions a pretext for
measures that would have been better left
undone, but for none that were of a sort to
establish confidence between the different
communities of mankind.—Whoever is under the belief that the social necessities of
the time played no part amongst the immediate causes of the present world-catas-

trophe, should ask himself this question:—
What direction would political impulses
have taken in the States that were rushing
into mutual war, if the "statesmen" had
recognised the social needs of the times,
and embodied these in their aims?   And
how much that was done would have been
left undone, if their efforts had thus been
directed to something more substantial
than piling up inflammable material, that
was bound sooner or later to lead to an
explosion?   As one watched the relations
between the States during recent years, and
the cancer creeping on in them, owing to
the form that social life had taken amongst
the leading sections of mankind, one could
understand how a man of broadly human
spiritual interests, such as Hermann
Grimm, was led to speak as he did, so early
in 1888, when discussing the form that
social aims had taken amongst the leading
circles:—"The end they set before them, is
the ultimate formation of mankind into
a commonwealth of brothers, who ever
afterwards shall go forward hand-in-hand,

actuated only by the noblest impulses. Merely to follow history on the map of Europe, one would imagine that a general internecine massacre were the next step imminent." Only the thought, that a "road must be found" to the true riches of human life, this thought alone can keep alive a sense of human worth. It is a thought "which hardly seems compatible with the gigantic preparations for war that we and our neighbours too are making. And yet, I believe in it. And in the light of this thought we must live; unless indeed it were better to put an end to human existence altogether by common consent, and appoint an official day of universal suicide" (Herman Grimm: "The Last Five Years,"—Pub. 1888.)—What were these "preparations for war," save steps taken by men who were bent upon preserving their old State constructions in one and un-divided form, despite the fact that the evo-lution of the new age had made this onefold form incompatible with the very essence of healthy relations between the peoples.

Health can, nevertheless, be brought into the common life of the peoples, by that form of social order that takes its shape from the requirements of the times.

The State-structure of Austria-Hungary had, for more than half a century, been struggling towards a new formation. Its spiritual life, which had its roots in a multiplicity of racial communities, called for a form of development to which the old onefold State, created by outworn impulses, offered a continual obstacle. The incident with which the great catastrophe opened— the quarrel between Austria and Serbia— is a conclusive sign, that the political frontiers of the onefold State ought not, after a certain point of time, to have formed the cultural frontiers for the spiritual life of its various nationalities. Could the spiritual life have been on its own footing, independent of the political State and political boundaries, it would have had a chance to develope regardless of frontiers, in a manner befitting the true purpose of the several nationalities; and the struggle,

which was deeply rooted in the spiritual
life, need never have found vent in a political catastrophe. Deliberate development
in this direction seemed an utter impossibility, sheer lunacy indeed, to all "statesman-like" thinkers in Austria-Hungary.
Their habits of thought admitted of no
other conception than that the boundaries
of State must also be the boundaries of
national community. They could not understand, how spiritual organisations could
be formed, cutting across state frontiers,
and comprising the school system and other
branches of spiritual life. It was against
all their habitual conceptions. And yet
this "inconceivable" thing is what international life demands in the new age. A
really practical thinker ought not to be
held up by apparent impossibilities, and
assume that the obstacles in the way of
doing what is requisite are insurmountable.
He must simply concentrate on surmount-
ing them. But instead of turning their
statesman-like thought along lines that
would have been in unison with modern-

age requirements, they devoted their whole energies to bolstering up the onefold form of State against the demands of the age by all manner of institutions. The State grew more and more unwieldy and impossible in its structure. And in the second decade of the twentieth century, it had reached a point when it could no longer keep itself together in its old form, and must either passively await dissolution, or else attempt to accomplish externally by force the internally impossible, and maintain itself by the power which a war-footing would give to it. In 1914 there remained for the Austro-Hungarian "statesmen" but one alternative:—Either they must direct their policy along the lines of life in a healthy social order, and make known their intention to the world,—a course which might have revived new confidence,—or else they were absolutely obliged to start a war, in order to keep the old structure from tumbling about their ears.—What happened in 1914 must be judged from these underlying causes; otherwise it is impossible to think correctly and justly about the question of "blame." The fact that many nationalities went to compose the fabric of her State, might well seem to have made it Austria-Hungary's mission in the world's history to lead the way in evolving a healthy form of social order. The mission was not recognised. And this sin against the spirit of the world's historic life drove Austria-Hungary into war.

And what about the German Empire?— The German Empire was founded at a moment, when the call of the new age for the healthy form of social life was endeavouring to find practical realisation. To have realised it, might have given the empire a justification for its existence in the world's history. All the social impulses met together in this realm of Central Europe, as if it were the ground allotted to them from of old in the world's history for them to work themselves out. The social tendency in thought was to be found in any number of places, but within the German Empire it assumed a form that plainly shewed whither it was tending. Here lay the work which should have given the empire its substance and purport. Here was the field of labour for those who were at the head of its affairs. This empire would have required no justification in the community of modern nations, had it received at its foundation a task and purport such as the forces of history themselves seemed to suggest. But instead of dealing with the task on a scale corresponding to its magnitude, those at the head of affairs contented themselves with "social reforms" arising out of the exigencies of the hour, and were delighted when such reforms as these were held up as models by other countries. And all the time, they were more and more seeking to establish the external prestige of the empire upon a pattern taken from the antiquated conceptions of the power and glory of States. They went on building up an empire, which was as contrary as the Austro-Hungarian fabric to everything that history shewed to be an active force in the modern life of the peoples. But of these forces the empire's governors saw nothing. The particular form of State-structure, that *they* had in their mind's eye, could only rest on military force. Whereas the form of State, that modern history demanded, must have rested on a practical realisation of the impulses that were making for a healthy social organism. In giving these impulses practical realisation, they would have made themselves a different place in the community of peoples from the position they actually occupied in 1914. Through failure to understand what was demanded by the life of the peoples in this new age, German policy had, in 1914, reached a dead-point as regards any possibility of further action. For years past, German policy had been blind to everything that ought to have been accomplished; it had busied itself with every conceivable thing that lay outside the forces of modern evolution, and that was bound inevitably from sheer hollowness to "tumble down like a house of cards."

The whole tragedy, thus brought about in the course of history and summed up in the fate of the German Empire, is to be found very faithfully reflected, for anyone who would take the trouble to examine and give the world a true and exact picture of what occurred in the leading quarters of Berlin in the last days of July and 1st August, 1914. Of these occurrences very little still is known, either at home or abroad. Whoever is acquainted with them knows, that German policy at that time was a card-house policy, that it had reached a dead-point in action; so that the whole question, as to whether there should be a war, or how it should begin, was inevitably made over to the decision of the military authorities. And the responsible people amongst the military authorities *could not,* from a military point of view, *act otherwise than they did act,* because *from that point of view,* the situation could only be regarded as they regarded it; for outside the military department things had got to a pass where no further action was possi-

ble.   This would be a notorious fact in
the world's history, if there were any
who would make it their business to bring
to light what went on in Berlin at the end
of July and on the first of August,—in particular on July 31 and August 1.   People
are still under the delusion, that nothing
is to be gained by a minute knowledge of
these occurrences, if one knows the pre-
vious events that led up to them.   But it is
knowledge that must not be shirked, if
there is to be any discussion of the question of "blame," as it is called to-day.   Of
course, there are other ways of arriving
at the causes, which were already of long
standing; but a detailed knowledge of these
few days reveals *the way in which these
causes acted.*

The notions, which at the time drove
Germany's leaders into war, continued
their baneful work.   They became the
mood of a nation.   And these same notions
prevented the people in power from acquiring by the bitter experiences of the final
terrible years that insight, for want of

which the tragedy had come about. These
experiences might well have opened men's
eyes; and, in this hope, the present writer
took what seemed to him an opportune moment in the war calamity, and did his best
to bring before various personages the
ideas underlying a healthy social organism,
and the political attitude that these entail
towards the world abroad. He addressed
himself to prominent individuals, whose influence at that time might still have been
exerted to carry these social impulses into
effect; and various persons, who had the
destiny of the German people honestly at
heart, took pains to gain admission for
these ideas. All that was said was in vain.
Every old habit of thought was up in arms
against social impulses of this kind, which
to a *purely military* cast of thought appeared quite impracticable,—something for
which they had no use at all. The farthest
they could get was: "Separation of Church
and School,"—yes,—there was something
in that. The thoughts of the "statesman-
like thinkers" had been running on lines

of that sort for years, and would not be
turned into any direction involving drastic
change.   Well-meaning people suggested
my "publishing" these proposals,—most
futile advise at that particular moment.
What would have been the good of another
treatise on these social impulses, in addition to all the other current literature of
the hour,—and coming from a private person too! From the very nature of such
impulses, they could, *at that time,* only have
carried weight through the quarter from
which they were pronounced. Had a pronouncement in favour of these impulses
been made from the right place, the peoples of Central Europe would have recognised the possibility of realising something
that was in sympathy with their own more
or less conscious tendencies. And the peoples of the Russian districts, East, would
at that time most undoubtedly have recognised in these social impulses a practical
solution to Czarism. That they could and
would have recognised the significance of
these impulses, is beyond dispute for any-

one able to perceive the as yet unexhausted intellectual vigour of the peoples of Eastern Europe, and how receptive their minds are to healthy social ideas. However, there was no pronouncement in favour of these ideas; and, instead, came Brest-Litovsk.

That military thinking could do nothing to avert the disaster from Central and Eastern Europe, could have been concealed from none but militarist minds. The cause of the German people's disaster was, that people would not recognise that the disaster could *not* be averted. They would not face the fact, that in those quarters, which had the deciding of affairs, there was no sense of the big, historic necessities. Anyone, who knew anything of these historic necessities, also knew, that the English - speaking races had persons amongst them, who were able to read the forces at work amongst the peoples of Central and Eastern Europe, and that these persons were convinced, that there was something working up in Central and Eastern Europe which must find vent in

tremendous social convulsions,—convulsions of a sort for which they believed there
to be no necessity nor occasion in the English-speaking regions. They framed their
own policy on these conclusions. In Central and Eastern Europe nothing was seen
of all this, and the people there shaped their
policy on lines which brought the whole
thing "like a house of cards" about their
ears. The only policy, which could have
had a solid foundation, would have been
one which recognised, that people in the
English-speaking countries were handling
the forces of world-history on large lines,
and of course, naturally, from the English
point of view. But to agitate in favour
of such a policy would have been regarded
as highly superfluous,—especially by the
"diplomatists."

So, instead of adopting a policy, which
might have also have ensured the prosperity of Central and Eastern Europe,—
despite the large lines of English policy,—
before the war-catastrophe swept over
everything, the leaders still continued to

run along the familiar diplomatic rails.
And, even amidst the horrors of war, bitter experience still failed to teach them,
when the manifesto came from America
announcing the world's mission in political terms, that it must be met by another
and a different one from Europe, born of
the forces of Europe herself. Wilson had
announced the world's mission from the
American standpoint. Europe's sense of
her mission would have been heard as a
spiritual impulse above the roar of the
guns. Between the two it would have been
possible to effect an understanding. All
other talk of mutual understanding rang
hollow in face of the historic necessities.
But those, whom circumstances brought to
the head of affairs in the German Empire,
lacked the perception which could make
them lay hold on the seeds of new growth
in modern human life and embody them in
a comprehensive aim. And, therefore, the
autumn of 1918 could bring nothing but
what it brought. The collapse of military
power was accompanied by spiritual sur-

render.   In this supreme hour, at least they might have roused themselves, have sought strength in the will and purpose of Europe, and made good the spiritual forces of the German people.   Instead, they abdicated to Wilson's Fourteen Points.   Wilson was confronted by a Germany that had nothing to say on her own account.   Whatever Wilson may think about his own 14 points, he is nevertheless powerless to help Germany except as Germany is willing. He was bound to await a pronouncement of her will.   The beginning of the war had already demonstrated the nullity of German policy.   It was again demonstrated in October, 1918.   So came that awful spiritual capitulation, at the hands of a man on whom numbers in German lands had staked as it were their last hope.

Want of faith in insight based on the forces at work through history;—unwillingness to seek strength in impulses that proceed from a perception of spiritual facts:—The state of Central Europe was due to these two things.

And now, to-day, the circumstances consequent on the war-catastrophe have created a new situation. The idea that gives its stamp to the new situation can be that of the social impulses of mankind, as conceived in this book. These social impulses speak a language, towards which the whole civilised world has a responsibility. Has thought spent itself, and come to its deadpoint before the social question as Central-European policy did before the problems of 1914? Some countries were able to stand aloof from the points that were then at issue. From the social movement they cannot stand aloof. This is a question that admits of no political adversaries and of no neutrals. Here, there must be but one human race working at one common task, willing to read the signs of the times and to act in accordance with them.

Lightning Source UK Ltd.
Milton Keynes UK
UKHW020928310123
416239UK00008B/414

9 781015 894662